# POLITICAL CAREERS
*Recruitment Through the Legislature*

# POLITICAL CAREERS
## Recruitment Through the Legislature

*Leonard Ruchelman*

FAIRLEIGH DICKINSON UNIVERSITY PRESS
*Rutherford* ▪ *Madison* ▪ *Teaneck*

Associated University Presses, Inc.
Cranbury, New Jersey 08512

The author wishes to thank Wayne State University Press
for permission to reprint "Lawyers in the New York Legislature: The Urban Factor," *Midwest Journal of Political Science,* Vol. X, No. 4, November, 1966, by Leonard Ruchelman.
Reprinted by permission of the Wayne State University Press.

SBN: 8386 7613 8

To my wife Diana

# CONTENTS

Preface                                                           11
Acknowledgments                                                   13

1. INTRODUCTION: LEGISLATORS AND "ELITE"
   THEORY                                                         19
   Legislative Decision-Makers as a "Political Elite"            20
   Theoretical perspective                                       22
   Political Careers and Research Design                         27
   The population                                                29
   Collection of data                                            31

2. THE CONSTITUENCY BASIS OF LEGISLATIVE
   RECRUITMENT                                                   33
   Malapportioned Constituencies                                 35
   Degree of Urbanization and Selected Background
   Characteristics                                               38
   Age and governmental experience                               38
   Legislative tenure                                            43
   Party and urbanization                                        48
   Legislators and Metropolitan Areas                            52
   Summation—Background Profiles                                 55

3. PATTERNS OF SOCIAL AND ETHNIC RE-
   CRUITMENT                                                     57
   Social Mobility                                               59
   Ethnic Recruitment                                            62
   Class Status                                                  66
   Class and parties                                             69
   Republican and Democratic lawyers                             70

7

Summary and Conclusion: The Circulation of
  Ethnic Elites                                                72

4. THE PROBLEM OF CONFLICTS OF INTEREST        75
  The Organizational Life of Legislators                       76
  Affiliations of Democrats and Republicans                    78
  Political Party Leadership                                   81
  Participation in Banking and Corporate Enterprise            83
  Occupational Interests                                       86
  Ethics and Legislators                                       88
  Conclusion: A Code of Ethics?                                92

5. ADIEU TO LEGISLATIVE OFFICE                 98
  How Legislators Leave                                        98
  Why Legislators Resign                                      100
    Political advancement                                     100
    The age cycle                                             101
  Defeat at the Polls                                         102
    The impact of national politics                           103
    The impact of reform politics                             105
    Finality of electoral defeat                              106
  Conclusion: The Consent of the Governed                     107

6. POST-LEGISLATIVE PATHWAYS                   111
  Post-Legislative Political Mobility                         113
  Where Do They Go in the Federal System?                     115
    National recruitment                                      115
    State recruitment                                         118
    City recruitment                                          119
    County recruitment                                        120
    Recruitment into other local units of government          121
  Where Do Legislators Go?—The Separate Branches
    of Government                                             122
    Legislative recruitment                                   123
    Executive recruitment                                     125
    Judicial recruitment                                      126
  The Bipolarization of Political Careers                     127
  Types of Careers                                            129
    Patron-Politicians                                        130
    Career-Politicians                                        134
    Amateur-Politicians                                       137

7. LAWYER-LEGISLATORS AND THE PURSUIT OF JUDGESHIPS — 139
  Lawyers as Career Politicians — 140
  Lawyers and Law-Enforcement Office — 142
    Law-enforcement experience — 142
    Law-enforcement mobility — 144
  The Urban Basis to the Dominance of Lawyers — 145
    Type of district and law-enforcement experience — 147
    New York City legislators: a tale of lawyers and judgeships — 148

8. LEGISLATIVE LEADERS — 152
  Elective Party Officers — 153
    The evolving pattern of legislative leadership — 154
  Committee Chairmen — 160
    A lesson in cultural lag — 161
  Career Strategy: Two Cases — 163
    The case of a small-town contender — 165
    The case of a big-city aspirant — 171
    Summation and conclusion — 175

9. CAREER BEHAVIOR AND THE FUNCTIONING OF THE POLITY — 179
  Career-Patterns and "Reality Worlds" — 180
    The Patrons—Protectors of the Old Order — 180
    The Careerists—"Politics as a Vocation" — 182
  Political Implications — 184
    Problem for Democracy: The Public Interest and the Private Interest — 185
    The Functional Role of Party — 186
    The Democratic party — 187
    The Republican party — 188
    Partisan Worlds — 189
    Relations with the Governor — 189
    Latent Aspects of Legislative Behavior — 191
    The "careerist" role vis à vis other roles — 192
    Manifest and latent consequences — 193
    Recommendations — 194

Bibliography — 197
Index — 213

# PREFACE

This book is an attempt to throw light on the careers of people who are recruited into politics—in this case, people who are recruited into New York legislative politics. We inquire as to who they are, where they come from, and where they go. The basic purpose of this study is not only to develop a better understanding of such persons, but also to better comprehend the political system in which they function. An inquiry of this kind can be made of just about any group of public officials in most political communities. I chose New York State legislators as my subject primarily because I have long been interested in the legislative process and, at the time of research, data on New Yorkers was most accessible.

Before proceeding to the material itself, I must first acknowledge a debt of gratitude to those who were of assistance to me and without whom this book would not have been possible. Professors David Truman, Wallace S. Sayre, and Malcolm Moos, with whom I worked as a graduate student at Columbia University, and Professor Luke Smith of Alfred University, all contributed many useful suggestions when this work was being prepared. I also wish to thank my former associates in the New York Metropolitan Region Program, Columbia University, who helped me think through many of my ideas and who were otherwise a source of comfort in times of stress. Peter Kidman and Howard G. Paster also provided valuable help in preparing and revising the manuscript.

11

Not to be overlooked is my wife, Diana, who showed immeasurable patience in reading and rereading all of my material to ascertain where my phrasing was "meaningful," a difficult task indeed.

LEONARD RUCHELMAN
Lehigh University
Bethlehem, Pa.

# ACKNOWLEDGMENTS

I would like to thank the following publishers for permission to reprint material from journal articles which I had previously written:

University of Utah, for permission to reprint excerpts from "A Profile of New York State Legislators," *Western Political Quarterly,* Vol. 20, No. 3, September 1967. Reprinted by permission of the University of Utah, copyright owners.

Wayne State University Press, for permission to reprint "Lawyers in the New York State Legislature: The Urban Factor," *Midwest Journal of Political Science,* Vol. 10, No. 4, November 1966. Reprinted by permission of Wayne State University Press.


I would also like to thank the following publishers for permission to quote from copyrighted material:

The American Academy of Political and Social Science, for permission to quote from Charles S. Hyneman, "Tenure and Turnover of Legislative Personnel," *The Annals,* Vol. 195, January 1938.

The American Political Science Association, for permission to quote from Daniel P. Moynihan and James Q. Wilson, "Patronage in New York State, 1955–1959," *American Political Science Review,* Vol. 48, No. 2, June 1964.

The University of Chicago Law Review, for permission to quote from Edward A. Shils, "The Legislator and His Environment," *The University of Chicago Law Review*, Vol. 18, Spring, 1951.

Columbia University Press, for permission to quote from Dixon Ryan Fox, *The Decline of Aristocracy in the Politics of New York*, 1919.

The Curtis Publishing Company, for permission to quote from Richard Armstrong, "Bobby Kennedy and the Fight for New York," *The Saturday Evening Post*, November 6, 1965. Reprinted with permission of the Saturday Evening Post, © 1965 Curtis Publishing Company.

Harcourt, Brace & World, Inc., for permission to quote from Edward N. Costikyan, *Behind Closed Doors*, 1966.

Alfred A. Knopf, Inc., for permission to quote from Richard Hofstadter, *The Age of Reform*, 1955; V. O. Key, *American State Politics*, 1956; William L. Riordan, *Plunkitt of Tammany Hall*, 1948.

McGraw-Hill Book Company, for permission to quote from Gaetano Mosca, *The Ruling Class*, edited by A. Livingston and translated by H. D. Kahn, 1939.

The M.I.T. Press, for permission to quote from Harold D. Lasswell, Daniel Lerner and C. E. Rothwell, *The Comparative Study of Elites*, Hoover Institute Studies, Series B, No. 1 (Stanford: Stanford University Press), 1952.

The Macmillan Company, for permission to quote from Daniel Bell, *The End of Ideology* (New York: Collier Books), 1962; and from Kingsley Davis, *Human Society*, 1949.

The New York Times Company, for permission to quote material from *The New York Times*, © 1950 and © 1967 by the New York Times Company. Reprinted by permission.

Oxford University Press, for permission to quote from H. H. Gerth and C. Wright Mills, eds., *From Max Weber,* 1946.

Prentice-Hall, Inc., for permission to quote from Belle Zeller, *Pressure Politics in New York: A Study of Group Representation Before the Legislature,* © 1937 Prentice-Hall, Inc.

Russell Sage Foundation, for permission to quote from Wallace S. Sayre and Herbert Kaufman, *Governing New York City,* 1960.

*Star-Gazette,* Elmira, N.Y. for permission to quote from *The Elmira Advertiser,* March 7, 1965.

The Viking Press, Inc., for permission to quote from Edward J. Flynn, *You're The Boss,* 1947.

John Wiley and Sons, Inc., for permission to quote from John C. Wahlke, Heinz Eulau, William Buchanan, and LeRoy C. Ferguson, *The Legislative System,* 1962.

I am also grateful to Warren Moscow for permission to quote from his book *Politics in the Empire State* (New York: Alfred A. Knopf, Inc.), 1948.

# POLITICAL CAREERS
*Recruitment Through the Legislature*

# 1

# INTRODUCTION: LEGISLATORS AND "ELITE" THEORY

Modern democratic governments assume many different forms, but all of them place special emphasis on the legislature as the principal means of realizing government by consent. Whether reference be made to the parliamentary system of fused powers or to the American scheme of separation of powers, it is in the legislative institution where "people" are represented, where the special interests of parties and groups most vividly confront one another, and where public policy is established by the enactment of law.

From the perspective of history, the legislature as a separate entity is a relatively modern phenomenon, having developed as democracy itself has developed. In truth, it can be said that the one is intimately dependent upon the other, perhaps to the point of survival. A key question, then, is how well do legislative bodies perform their responsibilities.

If the nineteenth century was the period of legislative supremacy, the twentieth century may yet bear witness to its undoing. Writing in 1885, Woodrow Wilson described how Congress dominated the President and Cabinet, even as to the details of administration.[1] But in 1908, Wilson took note of a new pattern: the Presidency was beginning

---

1. *Congressional Government* (New York: Meridian Books, 1956). First published in 1885.

to show its potential and Congress was no longer supreme.[2] On the state level as well as on the national level, legislative bodies have continued to evidence an almost unrelenting decline as the executive power has moved into the ascendancy.

In light of the growing complexity of problems which emanate from an increasingly urbanized society, this trend is perhaps unavoidable. For example, there are now more technical decisions which have to be delegated by law to bureaucrats in administrative agencies. At least equally significant is the fact that amateur legislators are no longer capable of dealing adequately with many of the intricate details of budgets; and by deferring on such matters to the experts in the executive branch they tend to abdicate an area which is fundamental to almost all subjects of policy-making. But, apart from this, a ready defense is less easily come by when other criticisms of legislative torpor and ineptitude are proffered. Of late, allegations of conflicts-of-interest, misrepresentation, high-pressure lobbying, procrastination and parochialism have grown louder and more persistent.[3] There are those who speculate whether, under present conditions, state government can even survive in any meaningful way.[4] Before we can more fully comprehend and prescribe remedies for these ills, however, we must develop new and more significant ways of perceiving legislative institutions and those who function within them.

## LEGISLATIVE DECISION-MAKERS AS A "POLITICAL ELITE"

There are many ways in which a legislative body can be analyzed, and if we look back through time it is possible

2. *Constitutional Government in the United States* (New York: Columbia University Press, 1908) .

3. For example, see James N. Miller, "Hamstrung Legislatures," *National Civic Review*, April, 1965, pp. 178–87, 219.

4. For example, see Charles Press and Charles R. Adrian, "Why Our State Governments Are Sick," *Antioch Review*, Summer, 1964, pp. 149–65.

to discern the different approaches. In the 1920s and 1930s, there was emphasis on the formal organizational machinery of lawmaking. Legal concepts and historicism were much the basis to explanation. For the most part, no real or systematic attempt was made to probe beneath the official, constitutional façade.

Immediately following World War II, greater attention was directed to the politics of legislative bodies. Interest groups and political parties were seen as major participants in lawmaking along with other contenders like the governor.[5] To convey insights into the dynamics of this process, the case study was developed as a technique of research.[6] Carrying this orientation further, political scientists have come to borrow a great deal from the sociologists: they strive to generalize about political behavior in the context of social interaction. The legislature itself is studied as a social system where lawmakers not only fulfill formal roles as determined by their official positions, e.g., committee chairman, Speaker, but normative roles as well, i.e., the fulfillment of widely held or self-held expectations of what a member must or should do.[7]

But if we are to understand how politicians act and react in an institutional setting, we must know more about them than we do at present. Among the questions to be asked are: Who are they? Where do they come from? Where are they going? This is the focus of the present book which analyzes New York State legislators.

---

5. A path-breaker was David B. Truman's book *The Governmental Process* (New York: Alfred A. Knopf, 1951), especially chapters 12 and 13.

6. One of the early and best studies of this kind has been Stephen K. Bailey's book *Congress Makes a Law* (New York: Columbia University Press, 1951).

7. This is the scheme of a four-state project by John C. Wahlke, Heinz Eulau, William Buchanan, and LeRoy C. Ferguson, entitled *The Legislative System: Explorations in Legislative Behavior* (New York: John Wiley and Sons, 1962). Among the roles identified are those of "ritualist"—concern with the mechanics of legislating, "inventor"—creator of public policy, "tribune"—advocate of popular demands, "broker"—compromiser.

*Theoretical perspective*

In our attempt to learn about individuals who become political decision-makers, it is necessary to organize our data so that it can convey as much meaning as may be possible. With this in mind it would be useful to refer to some of the classical writings of political elites to see what theories can be gleaned for our own purposes.

The term "elite" has reference to persons who hold political power—either the formal governing officials or the less visible economic and cultural influentials. Discourses on this subject can be traced back to Plato's *The Republic* and Aristotle's *Politics* where ideas on the rulers and the ruled were developed as "ideal" constructs. Preoccupied with the question "Who should rule?" both philosophers sought leaders of excellence who could promote the moral and material interests of the community. Most pertinent, from our point of view, is their recognition that an elite must emerge, that is, a minority of the whole, to bear responsibility for the social order. Indeed, Plato tells us that "neither cities nor States nor individuals will ever attain perfection until the small class of philosophers . . . are providentially compelled, whether they will or not, to take care of the State, and until a like necessity be laid on the State to obey them. . . ."[8]

Plato and Aristotle wrote for the city-state in ancient Greece. Given our interests in the present monograph, we must consider elite theories which are more directly relevant to modern, industrial societies. Indeed, the twentieth century heralded in a new group of scholars who attempted systematically to analyze "elites" and "masses" as a new approach to the study of politics. First among these was Gaetano Mosca, whose theory of the ruling class begins with the following statement:

Among the constant facts and tendencies that are to be found in all political organisms, one is so obvious that it

8. *The Republic,* Book VI, Jowett translation, p. 499.

is apparent to the most casual eye. In all societies—from societies that are very meagerly developed and have barely attained the dawning of civilization, down to the most advanced and powerful societies—two classes of people appear—a class that rules and a class that is ruled. The first class, always the less numerous, performs all political functions, monopolizes power and enjoys the advantages that power brings, whereas the second, the more numerous class, is directed and controlled by the first, in a manner that is now more or less legal, now more or less arbitrary and violent. . . .[9]

The power of the minority can be attributed to the fact that it is organized while the majority is not. Moreover, the minority is usually composed of high-status individuals: they ". . . regularly have some attribute, real or apparent, which is highly esteemed and very influential in the society in which they live."[10] To illustrate, warriors will dominate in a warlike society, farmers in an agrarian society. In so reflecting respected communal values, the ruling classes have a rationale by which they can better justify their authority.

Nor does Mosca believe that the principle of ruling elites is attenuated in representative systems of government. "When we say that the voters 'choose' their representative, we are using a language that is very inexact. The truth is that the representative *has himself elected* by the voters, and, if that phrase should seem too inflexible and too harsh to fit some cases, we might qualify it by saying that his friends *have him elected*. In elections, as in all other manifestations of social life, those who have the will and, especially, the moral, intellectual and material *means* to force their will upon others take the lead over the others and command them."[11] It can be said at this point that such disparagement of democratic methods

9. Gaetano Mosca, *The Ruling Class*, edited by A. Livingston and translated by H. D. Kahn (New York: McGraw-Hill Book Co., 1939), p. 50.
10. *Ibid.*, p. 53.
11. *Ibid.*, p. 154.

is worthy of careful investigation and will be a matter of interest in the present inquiry.

Like Mosca, Vilfredo Pareto classifies society into two major divisions: the "governing elite" and the lower stratum or "non-elite." But he also refers to another group within the top stratum which he labels the "non-governing elite."[12] The two leadership types are distinguished from each other primarily by their psychological traits. One type, the "speculators" (similar to Machiavelli's "foxes"), manifests the "instinct of combinations," a special talent for manipulation. They live by their wits and depend on fraud, deceit, and shrewdness. The other type, the "rentiers" (similar to Machiavelli's "lions"), though not very clever, are men of force. They tend to be patriotic and conservative, attaching great weight to tradition. Evidencing differences in outlook and leadership style, "rentiers" and "speculators" compete for the command positions. One type dominates only to the extent that existing social and political conditions are suitable for it. As society changes and new problems arise, different leadership skills are necessitated, e.g., force rather than manipulation. In this way, one personality type comes to replace the other. Thus Pareto formulates his theory of the "circulation of the elites." He contends that a relatively free circulation of the elites is necessary for a healthy society. When the elite becomes closed, or nearly closed, that society is threatened with internal revolution or with destruction from external forces.

Mosca also refers to the phenomenon of rotation of ruling groups, but unlike Pareto he does not attribute much importance to psychological factors. He highlights, rather, the emergence of new social forces and thus new interests. "If a new source of wealth develops in a society, if the practical importance of knowledge grows, if an old

---

12. Vilfredo Pareto, *The Mind and Society*, edited and translated by A. Livingston (New York: Harcourt, Brace and World, 1935), 4 vols. See 3:1422–24.

religion declines or a new one is born, if a new current of ideas spreads, then, simultaneously, far-reaching dislocations occur in the ruling class."[13]

Harold Lasswell is a more contemporary scholar who follows in the tradition of Pareto and Mosca, especially the latter.[14] In the Hoover Institute Studies on elites, he and his associates define the political elite in the following terms.[15]

> The political elite comprises the power holders of a body politic. The power holders include the leadership and the social formations from which leaders typically come, and to which accountability is maintained, during a given generation. In other words, the political elite is the top power class. Obviously, it does not include all members of the body politic unless everyone shares equally in the decision process. The extent of power sharing must be determined in every situation by research, since there is no universal pattern of power. We speak of an *open elite* when all or a very considerable number of the members of a body politic are included. A *closed elite*, on the other hand, embraces only a few.

Lasswell differs from his predecessors in that he is preoccupied with the elite as they serve in institutions of government. This is not to say that other elites, e.g., business or military leaders, may not have some or even most of the decision-making authority; but "since the true decision-makers are not necessarily known at the beginning of research, the investigator can select government in the conventional sense as a convenient starting point."[16]

Furthermore, Lasswell, like the others, is interested in elite transformations, but he is more systematic in his

---

13. Mosca, p. 65.
14. Lasswell's early writings were commended by Mosca himself.
15. Harold D. Lasswell, Daniel Lerner and C. E. Rothwell, *The Comparative Study of Elites*, Hoover Institute Studies, Series B, no. 1 (Stanford: Stanford University Press, 1952), p. 13.
16. Lasswell, *ibid.*, p. 8.

attempt to account for the effects of basic cultural forces. Industrialization, the decreasing number of great national powers in the world community, and the continuing crisis of world insecurity have all affected political leaders in important ways. The emergence of such conditions over time, he explains, has changed recruitment patterns. As the old pre-industrial aristocrats declined due to new technological developments, businessmen were elevated to positions of authority. But this pattern was soon diluted in the face of rising political tensions and, consequently, the professional politicians—experts on persuasion and manipulation—have come to supplant the business groups. Lasswell anticipates that if the world crisis continues, specialists in persuasion will be replaced by specialists in coercion, i.e., those with skill in handling tools of violence.

It is these theorists, then—Mosca, Pareto, and Lasswell— who provide us with an agenda of inquiry in the present study of a political elite. Such matters as who is recruited into political office, i.e., their social status, skills and competence, how representative they are of the larger community, the rate and special qualities of personnel circulation, are all derived from their writings. We borrow, moreover, another related concept: patterns of elite recruitment both reflect and affect society. On the one hand, the history and character of a body politic can be understood from insights into the composition of its elite; as the polity changes, as new social groups form and new values come into play, so it is that leaders change. On the other hand, as an independent factor, political elites influence policy in the community and thereby determine stability in the system, i.e., the way in which change is to be accommodated.

A major difference between the aforementioned treatises and this one is that the others have attempted to take in the broad sweep of things on a world-historical level of generalization. Our focus is considerably narrower. We study legislative personnel in the State of New York over a relatively limited period of time. By so confining our subject material, we hope to have some of the best of both worlds, namely, a rigorous, empirical investigation as well as the richness of at least a few fruitful hypotheses.[17]

## POLITICAL CAREERS AND RESEARCH DESIGN

This book is not only concerned with political recruitment—who comes into decision-making positions—but it also focuses upon political careers, i.e., what happens to public officials during their political lifetime. More precisely, a political career can be defined as a pattern in the lives of men moving into different positions made available by the governmental framework. Important is the fact that career paths are not necessarily the result of mere chance; nor are they determined entirely by the skills of the politician. Rather, there is good reason to believe that, given certain conditions, career lines show important uniformities.

Of major significance is the way the social attributes of the politician affect political mobility. Here we are concerned with such data as the office-seeker's home constituency, occupational status, social origin, education level, and ethnic and religious character. These qualities have a bearing on what happens to him in the world of politics.

Another important variable is the way in which the political system is structured. To the extent that there

17. Other relatively recent expositions of political elites, similar to the present one, include: Donald R. Matthews, *The Social Background of Political Decision-Makers* (New York: Doubleday and Co.. 1954) and *U.S. Senators and Their World* (Chapel Hill: The University of North Carolina Press, 1960); Joseph Schlesinger, *Ambition and Politics: Political Careers in the United States* (Chicago: Rand McNally & Co., 1966); Dwaine Marvick. ed., *Political Decision-Makers: Recruitment and Performance* (New York: The Free Press of Glencoe, 1961); Austin Ranney, *Pathways to Parliament* (Madison & Milwaukee: The University of Wisconsin Press, 1965).

is variation in the system, career opportunities vary as well. A political role which is successfully performed in one type of community may prove to be entirely inadequate in another. The kind of data we are most concerned with here pertains to such factors as the availability of different types of governmental positions, the functions performed by political parties and organized groups, and the formal means of political movement, e.g., nominations, elections and appointments.

This study of the careers of New York State legislators may be characterized as having three related stages:[18]

1. Recruitment into the legislature: On the basis of our review of some major theories of political elites, we can expect that a thorough scrutiny of those who share power in the New York Legislature would be revealing in a number of ways. First, in discerning who is accorded prestige by membership in the lawmaking body, we can assess the values of the cultural environment of New York. For example, if business interests play a central role in the state, it is likely that more businessmen than farmers or laborers would be chosen for positions of authority. Second, changes in the composition of the legislature are clues to social change. As new groups in society assert themselves, it can be assumed that they would want a greater share in formal lawmaking. Third, in comparing members of the legislature with the general population, we are able to determine the extent to which the lawmakers are indeed representative of society. Fourth, the attitudes and behavior of public office-holders are in many ways influenced by their personal life histories. Thus a study of the background characteristics of legislators can help substantially in conveying insights into the nature of legislative decision-making.

---

18. For expository purposes, the organization of chapters do not follow this exact order. The first stage consists of Chapters 2 and 3, and 4. Chapters 5 and 6 are incorporated into the third stage. Chapter 7, which deals with the lawyer-legislator, overlaps the first and third; and Chapter 8 treats the second stage.

2. Recruitment within the legislature: Also investigated is the leadership core which functions within the legislative chambers. Among our interests here is the determination of who holds leadership positions, how the leaders change over time, and the extent to which they are representative of their legislative following. In addition, attention is directed to whether intra-legislative promotion is in some way significant for elevation into extra-legislative political office.

3. Recruitment out of the legislature: We not only focus upon the background characteristics of those who have arrived at a particular level in the governmental structure (i.e., the legislature), but we are also interested in what happens to such persons afterward. In effect we ask: What are the relevant qualities of those legislators who continue to ascend the political career ladder and how do they differ from those who stay put or who evidence signs of descent? Some clear answers here will permit us to generalize about politicians who fall by the wayside in the pursuit of a career as well as those who show achievement.

## The population

Why study the political mobility of state legislators? It is believed that an investigation of the careers of New York legislative personnel is a useful means of implementing our research goals. As Lester Seligman states it: "The position held most often in a political career is that of state legislator. It is thus the most important first rung on the ladder of political ascent. The position of state legislator has considerable potential for political mobility."[19]

In planning methodology, it was necessary to deal with the problem of how to measure the effects of social and political change upon the career paths of the legislators.

19. "Prefatory Study of Leadership Selection in Oregon," *Western Political Quarterly* 12 (March, 1959) :154.

Perhaps the ideal way of proceeding would be to observe the career lines of all legislators over a period of time, e.g., from 1930 to 1950. But a research project of such dimensions would be unmanageably large. Instead, it was decided that the memberships of two different legislative sessions should be investigated. A reasonable span of time was allowed to intervene between the sessions. In this way it was still possible to include a time variable, though in modified form. Furthermore, it should be noted that *the two samples are more inclusive than might appear to be the case at first glance;* this is because most of the legislators held their seats both before and after the particular legislative sessions chosen for study. (In 1951, for example, 75 percent of all lawmakers served for nine or more years.)

The two groups of lawmakers studied are those who convened in the years 1931 and 1951. Both are similar in that they evidenced a relatively low turnover of members and they had almost the same party apportionment. Also, the 1931 and 1951 lawmakers were elected at a time when the influence of a Presidential election was about two years away.[20] It is believed that these factors have helped make for reliable comparisons between the two samples.

The total number of lawmakers observed is 413. This consists of 201 members who served in 1931 and 206 who served in 1951, minus six who held seats through both sessions. In addition, there is the leadership bloc which includes all those who occupied the following offices from 1920 to 1966: Speaker, Majority Leader, and Minority Leader in the Assembly; President Pro Tem and Minority Leader in the Senate. This provides an additional population of 35. Since twenty of these, however, fall into the already mentioned grouping of 401 lawmakers, there are only fifteen more subjects that have been included. Thus the net population totals 416.

---

20. The legislative election dates were November 1930 and November 1950.

more of the population lives in places of 2,500 to 24,999;
(5) districts where 50 percent of more of the population
lives in places which have less than 2,500 people.[4] By so
establishing an urban-rural continuum, we hope to avoid
the oversimplifications which can result when town and
full-blown city are considered as sharply distinct categories.

## MALAPPORTIONED CONSTITUENCIES

The method of apportioning legislative districts is basic
to an understanding of "who" comes into the legislature.
The proportion of urban lawmakers in comparison to
rural lawmakers, the number of Democrats as opposed
to Republicans, the degree to which age and experience
prevail over youth and inexperience are, among other
things, all affected by the system of apportionment. Thus,
some reference to this matter must serve as a necessary
beginning to an analysis of our data.

Most significant is the fact that in New York, as well
as in most states of the Union, there has existed an approach to districting wherein the rural constituencies have
been overrepresented while the most urbanized ones have
been underrepresented. The history of the state reveals
two techniques as having been primarily responsible for
such unbalanced representation: state constitutional restrictions and the failure of the legislature to reapportion
seats as the population changed. Toward the end of the
nineteenth century, the rapid growth of cities, especially
New York City, portended a shift in power away from

4. A necessary qualification to our method of classifying constituencies
must be noted. Some legislators who served in 1951 were found to represent districts which were below the 2,500 population limit but were
nevertheless considered urban as based upon the 1950 Census definition
of urban areas. They were in the densely settled urban fringe surrounding
cities of 50,000 inhabitants or more. These districts were placed in the
2,500-plus class. This was necessitated by the fact that they did not provide
enough legislators to warrant a separate category; yet, because of their
more urban qualities, they could not be considered comparable to the
most rural districts.

the small towns and the outlying countryside. The enfranchisement of multitudes of propertyless workers, moreover, who inhabited the large urban centers alarmed men of property throughout the state, urban as well as rural. "The average citizen in the rural districts," said a delegate to the New York State Constitutional Convention of 1894, "is superior in intellect, superior in morality, superior in self-government to the average citizen of the great cities." Because most of his fellow delegates agreed with him, they wrote apportionment formulas into the Constitution strategically designed to give the virtuous country man a commanding voice in the legislature. The basic membership in the Assembly was permanently fixed at 150 seats. This restriction and the fact that each county, irrespective of size, was given at least one representative in that house (except Fulton and Hamilton counties which were to count as one), was enough to insure that New York City would be denied its proportionate share of representation. In the Senate, more complicated provisions were established. Membership was set at 50 seats and the size of the house could increase when a county qualified for additional representation by reason of growing population. But the Senate formula made it difficult for large counties to gain and keep additional representation. Among other things, no county could have a fourth Senator unless such county had at least eight percent of the state's total citizen population (five Senators were to be justified by ten percent of the state's citizen population, etc.). In addition, the provision for enlarging the Senate resulted in over-representation of the rural counties. Whenever the population of the most crowded counties increased so that it was entitled to more Senators, the additional seats were not taken from the less populous counties even though their proportion of the state's citizen population may have decreased.

From 1919 to 1942, there was no reapportionment de-

spite the constitutional mandate that it be effected every
ten years after the Federal Census. Political battles between Democratic governors and the Republican-con-
trolled legislature and, in 1935, between a Democratic
governor and a Democratic-controlled legislature, pre-
vented change. Even with reapportionment in succeeding
years (1943, 1953, 1961), the 1894 provisions still per-
tained, resulting in considerable acrimony between leaders of New York City and upstate. Augmenting the problem were massive postwar population shifts. The suburbs
boomed and soon became additional victims of malapportionment. Large cities found they were losing many of
their middle-class residents to the suburbs while at the
same time receiving new migrant peoples of limited skills
and resources. Rural places lost population. It wasn't
until June 15, 1964, that a major breakthrough was
achieved in the Supreme Court decision *WMCA, Inc. v.
Lomenzo, Secretary of State of New York*. Overruling a
lower federal court, the nation's highest tribunal declared
that representation in both houses of the New York State
Legislature must be based on population. Speaking for
the Court, Justice Warren stated: "However complicated
or sophisticated an apportionment scheme might be, it
cannot, consistent with the Equal Protection Clause, result in a significant undervaluation of the weight of the
votes of certain of a state's citizens merely because of
where they happen to reside." Because of the built-in
bias against voters living in the more populous counties,
he continued, "legislative representation accorded to the
urban and suburban areas becomes proportionately less
as the population of these areas increases."[5] As illustration
of Warren's contention, Table 1 provides some measure-
ment of representation by district size for the years 1931

5. 377 U.S. 653. It should be noted that nothing was said in this case
about gerrymandering, the technique by which district boundaries are
drawn in such a way as to give one political party or faction advantage
over another.

and 1951. Just how this rural bias affected the legislative membership is the next stage of analysis. In the long run we shall also be interested in how such malapportionment continues to affect the larger political system of New York State, especially in terms of its leadership in the 1960s and 1970s.

Table 1. Urban-Rural Representation by Districts.

| Type of district | 1930 population | 1931 legislators | 1950 population | 1951 legislators |
|---|---|---|---|---|
| New York City | 55% | 42% | 53% | 45% |
| | | N 85 | | N 92 |
| 100,000+ | 12% | 13% | 10% | 11% |
| | | N 26 | | N 23 |
| 25,000+ | 6% | 9% | 7% | 8% |
| | | N 19 | | N 17 |
| 2,500+ | 11% | 10% | 15% | 14% |
| | | N 21 | | N 29 |
| —2,500 | 16% | 25% | 15% | 22% |
| | | N 50 | | N 45 |
| Total | 100% | 99% | 100% | 100% |
| | | N 201 | | N 206 |

## DEGREE OF URBANIZATION AND SELECTED BACKGROUND CHARACTERISTICS

*Age and governmental experience*

From the data in Table 2, it can be generalized that the more urban the district the younger the legislator and the more rural the district the older the legislator. This can be attributed to the fact that most rural lawmakers contribute a great many of their youthful years to service in local government. Such qualities are in sharp contrast to New York City personnel, a large majority of whom show no prior activity in public office. We should note, also, that legislators who come from the next most urban districts—100,000 plus—are not nearly as inexperienced.

One explanation for this, but by no means the whole explanation, is that there are many more political positions available in the outlying rural areas. An abundance of governmental units in the form of counties, villages, towns, school districts and small cities provides numerous opportunities to the public office-seeker.[6] Also relevant are basic communal values intrinsic to small-town America. The aspiring leader is expected to serve an apprenticeship in local affairs because, it is alleged, little government, as distinguished from large, "bureaucratic" systems, is desirable and good. The rewards of such service are "found in the virtue of the people, the openness and forthrightness of public transactions, and the simplicity of governmental machinery."[7] It can be assumed that the political newcomer in smaller communities who doesn't defer to such grass-roots ideas would find it quite difficult to begin a public career.

The failure of most New York City personnel to show

---

6. There is no authoritative count to show the number of elective and appointive public offices in New York State. However, it would be helpful to note the number of government units which exist. A United States Census Report for 1957 shows that, outside of New York City, there are 57 counties, 61 cities, 932 towns, 550 villages, 1,664 school districts and 921 special districts. All of these units provide an abundance of political positions. For a rough outline of the kinds of elective offices available in these governmental bodies, see United States Bureau of the Census, *United States Census of Government: 1957*, vol. 6, no. 30, *Government in New York* (Washington: Government Printing Office, 1959), Table 9. Within New York City, there are five counties and three special districts, *ibid.*, Table 8. Wallace Sayre and Herbert Kaufman estimate that the city provides about 350 elective positions and about 1,000 key appointive offices, *Governing New York City* (New York: Russell Sage Foundation, 1960), p. 44.

7. Roscoe C. Martin, *Grass Roots: Rural Democracy in America* (Alabama: University of Alabama Press, 1957), p. 31. For a full description of the expression of small-town values in an upstate New York community, see Arthur J. Vidich and Joseph Bensman, *Small Town in Mass Society* (Garden City, New York: Anchor Books, Doubleday & Co., 1958).

Table 2. Age and Governmental Experience of 1931 and 1951 Legislators According to Type of District.

| Selected Characteristics | New York City | 100,000+ | 25,000+ | 2,500+ | —2,500 | All legis-lators |
|---|---|---|---|---|---|---|
| **Age of legislators** | | | | | | |
| —35 years | | | | | | |
| 1931 | 42% | 39% | 11% | 10% | 8% | 27% |
| 1951 | 13 | 13 | 6 | 3 | 4 | 9 |
| 36-45 years | | | | | | |
| 1931 | 32 | 19 | 26 | 19 | 18 | 24 |
| 1951 | 48 | 44 | 35 | 14 | 13 | 24 |
| 46-55 years | | | | | | |
| 1931 | 8 | 27 | 26 | 24 | 32 | 20 |
| 1951 | 35 | 30 | 41 | 35 | 29 | 34 |
| 56-65 years | | | | | | |
| 1931 | 14 | 12 | 21 | 43 | 30 | 21 |
| 1951 | 2 | 9 | 12 | 31 | 33 | 15 |
| 66+ years | | | | | | |
| 1931 | 2 | 4 | 16 | 5 | 8 | 6 |
| 1951 | 1 | — | — | 14 | 16 | 6 |
| Unknown | | | | | | |
| 1931 | 1 | — | — | — | 4 | 2 |
| 1951 | 1 | 4 | 6 | 3 | 4 | 3 |
| Total | | | | | | |
| 1931 | 99% | 101% | 100% | 101% | 100% | 101% |
| 1951 | 100% | 100% | 100% | 100% | 99% | 101% |
| | | | | | | |
| **Governmental experience*** | | | | | | |
| None | | | | | | |
| 1931 | 87% | 58% | 16% | 38% | 36% | 59% |
| 1951 | 67 | 39 | 18 | 35 | 31 | 48 |
| Local† | | | | | | |
| 1931 | 7 | 23 | 68 | 48 | 52 | 27 |
| 1951 | 7 | 52 | 59 | 62 | 60 | 35 |
| City | | | | | | |
| 1931 | 4 | 15 | 26 | 10 | 4 | 8 |
| 1951 | 10 | 13 | 41 | 7 | 4 | 11 |

State
| | | | | | | |
|---|---|---|---|---|---|---|
| 1931 | 2 | 8 | — | — | 4 | 4 |
| 1951 | 9 | 4 | 6 | 3 | 13 | 8 |

National
| | | | | | | |
|---|---|---|---|---|---|---|
| 1931 | 1 | — | 5 | 5 | 12 | 5 |
| 1951 | 15 | — | — | 3 | 7 | 9 |

Elective‡
| | | | | | | |
|---|---|---|---|---|---|---|
| 1931 | 1 | 27 | 79 | 43 | 50 | 28 |
| 1951 | 1 | 44 | 71 | 59 | 58 | 32 |

Appointive‡
| | | | | | | |
|---|---|---|---|---|---|---|
| 1931 | 12 | 23 | 26 | 24 | 26 | 19 |
| 1951 | 33 | 22 | 29 | 28 | 34 | 29 |

* Percentages do not total up to 100 percent since a legislator could be counted two or three or four times if he previously held positions on two, three or four levels of government.

† This refers to village, town and special district government.

‡ A legislator was counted twice if he previously served in both elective and appointive positions.

prior public service appears to contradict the general assumption that state leaders usually undergo governmental grooming and testing at some earlier stage in their careers. As an illustration of such a viewpoint, note an official report to the Commission on Inter-Governmental Relations: "The counties, cities, towns, villages and boroughs serve as training schools for the leaders of government and in the affairs of local government are tried those who aspire to State and National office."[8] In reality, as shown by our New York statistics, a majority of all 1931 legislators and close to half of the 1951 group were political outsiders.

It should be noted, however, that some change has taken place. More 1951 big-city politicians were able to show pre-legislative experience than was previously the case. Interestingly, a greater proportion of them served on the national level rather than in the city as might be

8. *Local Government,* a report by the Advisory Committee on Local Government to the Commission on Inter-Governmental Relations (Washington: U.S. Government Printing Office, 1955), p. 9.

expected. But, in spite of this tendency, New York City lawmakers have continued to manifest a near complete lack of elective experience; almost always, pre-legislative positions, minimal as they are, are appointive ones. This can be accounted for by the dearth of elective offices, other than state legislative seats, in the metropolis. Another reason is that it is the party club, rather than local elective office, which introduces the urban person to politics. That is to say, the fledgling politician in a place like New York City doesn't have to acquire prominence by running for the city council prior to a try for the state legislature: this would be superfluous. Instead, the very first step is to gain the approval of the leaders and members of the local club—approval which is based primarily on organization standards. As told by the former leader of Manhattan's Tammany Hall: ". . . club members, captains, club officers, and leaders together reach a consensus on the candidate based on a variety of factors—such as past service and performance, personality, friendship, loyalty, capacity to campaign, judgment and intelligence, capacity to finance a campaign (and perhaps to finance the local clubs after the campaign) ."[9] Upon acceptance, the political aspirant can either be recommended for appointment to an administrative slot or designated for party nomination to an elective position.[10]

Accordingly, the upstate legislator derides his metropolitan colleague for lacking the "proper credentials" and for his dependence on the party machine. The following comments are typical:

9. The statement in parenthesis is part of the quote. See Edward N. Costikyan, *Behind Closed Doors: Politics in the Public Interest* (New York: Harcourt, Brace and World, Inc., 1966) , p. 103. Sayre and Kaufman define a political club as ". . . a voluntary association of party members, an unofficial, self-governing society of individuals. A club is forbidden by the Election Law to identify itself publicly with a party unless authorized to do so by the party's county executive committee." P. 137.

10. Once designated, the candidate runs in the party primary—an intra-party election. More often than not, a heavy turn-out of party regulars as voters assures the nomination.

There are many young . . . assemblymen downstate and their only experience politically was probably as party workers in their own ward or district. They have no political background to speak of.

I really think that nobody can get on the ticket in New York City unless he has come through the (party) ranks and has the bosses and organization behind him. I talked to one fellow who went to a caucus expecting to go to Congress. That was turned down. He (was told) he could not go to the state Senate and he wound up in the Assembly.[11]

Though defenders of the classical concept of grass-roots democracy find it difficult to understand, clubhouse involvement may be the only feasible way for the politician to interact with both prospective voters and fellow political activists in a large, impersonal, urban setting. Such participation, moreover, can be considered a form of community activity more closely related to grass-roots phenomena than is ordinarily supposed. According to Theodore Lowi: "Many District organizations are in actual fact 'bunde,' or at least fraternities, modern vestiges of the fraternal-convivial origins of Tammany Hall, the neighborhood gangs, the ghettos, and the self-defensive societies of new national groupings."[12] It is generally the case that emerging communal forces—whether they be middle-class reformers challenging "old-guard" elements or new ethnic groups seeking to replace older, established ones—are channeled through these very same organizations.[13]

## Legislative tenure

It is commonly observed that a legislative body cannot function effectively unless a substantial number of its

---

11. The Elmira *Advertiser,* March 7, 1965.
12. Theodore J. Lowi, *At the Pleasure of the Mayor* (New York: The Free Press of Glencoe, 1964) , p. 180.
13. For a rather thorough analysis of this see James Q. Wilson, *The Amateur Democrat: Club Politics in Three Cities* (Chicago: The University of Chicago Press, 1962) .

Table 3. Tenure: Number of Sessions in the Legislature, 1931 and 1951 Legislators Compared According to Type of District.

| Tenure in years | New York City | 100,000+ | 25,000+ | 2,500+ | —2,500 | All legis-lators |
|---|---|---|---|---|---|---|
| 1-4 yrs. | | | | | | |
| 1931 | 13% | 12% | 37% | 10% | 10% | 14% |
| 1951 | 13 | 4 | 6 | 3 | 4 | 8 |
| 5-8 yrs. | | | | | | |
| 1931 | 29 | 50 | 32 | 29 | 38 | 34 |
| 1951 | 20 | 26 | 18 | 14 | 7 | 16 |
| 9-12 yrs. | | | | | | |
| 1931 | 33 | 19 | 21 | 29 | 16 | 25 |
| 1951 | 17 | 4 | 12 | 3 | 13 | 13 |
| 13-16 yrs. | | | | | | |
| 1931 | 16 | 15 | 11 | 19 | 18 | 16 |
| 1951 | 20 | 35 | 41 | 31 | 24 | 26 |
| 17+ yrs. | | | | | | |
| 1931 | 8 | 4 | — | 14 | 18 | 10 |
| 1951 | 30 | 30 | 23 | 48 | 51 | 37 |
| Total | | | | | | |
| 1931 | 99 | 100 | 101 | 101 | 100 | 99 |
| 1951 | 100% | 100% | 100% | 99% | 99% | 100% |

NOTE: Members of the Assembly were elected for one year terms until 1938 when, in accordance with a constitutional amendment adopted in 1937, the term was increased to two years. Tenure is accounted for up to the 1966 session.

members are seasoned enough in the business of lawmaking. Using this criterion, New York lawmakers score quite high. The information available in Table 3 indicates that there are very few who served for as little as four sessions. In all, approximately 85 percent of the 1931 legislators and about 92 percent of the 1951 legislators held their seats for five or more sessions.

It is also evident that those who are from New York City districts were not serving for as long a time as other representatives. Having arrived at a relatively youthful age with little or no previous experience, big-city politicians are evidently intent on moving through the legislative chambers at a faster pace. Differences in tenure, moreover, between New York City persons and those who represent the most rural places seem to have become greater over time.

There are some sound reasons for the more rapid come-and-go of the urbanites. Until 1960, New York City legislators represented a majority of the state's population; yet, in the legislature, they have amounted to no more than a minority bloc in confrontation with other blocs often united against them. Opportunities for prominence have been limited as intra-legislative promotions, e.g., committee chairmanships, the Speakership, go to others who are affiliated with the majority.

Of additional significance is the group life of the legislature. Like any other functioning group, the New York legislative body has informal norms and practices which make it more comfortable for the long-standing member as against the relative newcomer. Consider the following testimony:

> . . . in the Legislature, we have what is known as a Ten-Year Club. This is an organization of legislators who are in the State Legislature for a minimum of ten years, and this is a powerful club, made up of Democrats and Republicans. And if you are a member of this club, you can call upon your colleagues who are also members of this club for various types of friendly reaction to problems.[14]

It can be assumed from our data that many more rural persons have been eligible for membership to this inner group than have been urban lawmakers.

Over-all, malapportionment tended to assure an up-

---

14. Ludwig Teller (a former legislator), "Reminiscences." Columbia University Oral History Collection, Special Collections, Butler Library, p. 237.

state, small-town atmosphere for the legislative process; and while it perhaps has been friendly, even convivial (as many have testified), the man who represents the large urban center has been apt to find legislative service an unrewarding, at times frustrating experience. Now that a new system of district apportionment, as based on population, has been instituted by order of the United States Supreme Court, patterns of legislative tenure will probably begin to change.

Our data is revealing of another aspect of legislative tenure: namely, a substantially larger percentage of all 1951 lawmakers have held on in the legislature for a much longer time than their 1931 predecessors. In this respect, New York is succeeding where other states are failing.[15] The perplexing problem of high turnover in other legislatures is commented on by Charles S. Hyneman:

> The real task is to find why so many legislators, senators and representatives alike, choose not to run again. Devices and arrangements which reduce the hazards of an election year to a minimum will still not give us a body of lawmakers rich in the experience of their trade. The state legislator must be made more happy in his career. . . . The key to rehabilitation of the legislative branch is in the nature of the legislator's job and his attitude toward it.[16]

It can be suggested here that one major inducement which helps make the state legislator "more happy in his career" is his salary. During the 1930s and most of the 1940s, pay in New York was held to $2,500 a year. Considering growing inflation, especially during World War II, little pecuniary incentive was provided. According to Warren Moscow,

---

15. It was reported in 1954 that close to one-half of the approximately 7,600 legislators are replaced every two years due primarily to failure to run for re-election. See Belle Zeller, ed., *American State Legislatures* (New York: Thomas Y. Crowell Co., 1954), pp. 61, 65.

16. Charles S. Hyneman, "Tenure and Turnover of Legislative Personnel," *The Annals of the American Academy of Political and Social Science*, 195 (January, 1938):30–31.

this situation was especially burdensome to the city representatives. "To the retired farmer or grain and seed merchant from an upstate hamlet this salary ($2,500) was enough to pay him for his time. To the urban lawyer or insurance agent it was chicken-feed—about enough to pay his entertainment expenses during a dull session."[17] Consequently, a better offering somewhere else, publicly or privately, was often enough to encourage departure. Nor was there much hope for quick improvement, as the remuneration of legislators was fixed by the State Constitution; any change had to be made in the form of an amendment to be ratified by the citizenry. In 1947, however, the voters approved a referendum which canceled that provision, thus making it possible to upgrade salaries by a simple change in the law. The legislators took advantage of their new opportunity the following year by doubling their salaries from $2,500 to $5,000. The situation continued to improve thereafter, making New York one of the highest-paying states in the nation. In 1955, salaries were increased to $7,500 and in 1963 it went to $10,000. Most recently in 1966, the lawmakers approved another raise to $15,000 which went into effect in 1967.[18] Thus we see that steadily improving monetary rewards were made available to the 1952 personnel which were not available to the shorter-tenured 1931 group. Another reason, certainly, for shorter tenure on the part of the 1931 lawmakers is the fact that Assemblymen had to risk their seats annually rather than biennially as was the case beginning in 1938.

The public is not necessarily aware or appreciative of the idea that higher pay makes for more experienced

17. Warren Moscow, *Politics in the Empire State* (New York: Alfred A. Knopf, 1948), pp. 179–180.

18. In addition to regular annual salaries, New York legislators receive expense allowances which now amount to $3,000 a year. Legislative leaders get substantially more. Such lump-sum payments are referred to as "lulus" which is a slang term for payment "in lieu of" an itemized accounting of expenses.

representatives. Fearing reprisals at the polls, legislators move stealthily when enacting salary hikes for themselves. The last time this happened in 1966, the bill was introduced rather suddenly at the very end of the session over the July Fourth holiday weekend. To hasten procedures, the normal requirement that a bill must sit on legislators' desks for three days before it can be acted on was waived.

## Party and urbanization

Our urban-rural scale, not unexpectedly, reveals much less variation in the party affiliations of lawmakers than was the case in testing other variables, i.e., age, tenure, experience. As can be seen in Table 4, most of the Democrats come from New York City while the Republicans predominate in the rest of the state. Furthermore, this party division persists over time.

Table 4. Political Party Affiliation of 1931 and 1951 Legislators, Classified by Type of District.

| Type of District | 1931 legislators | | | 1951 legislators | | |
|---|---|---|---|---|---|---|
| | Dem. | Repub. | All | Dem. | Repub. | All |
| New York City | | | | | | |
| percent | 96% | 4% | 100% | 86% | 14% | 100% |
| number | 82 | 3 | 85 | 79 | 13 | 92 |
| 100,000+ | | | | | | |
| percent | 27% | 73% | 100% | 22% | 78% | 100% |
| number | 7 | 19 | 26 | 5 | 18 | 23 |
| 25,000+ | | | | | | |
| percent | 5% | 95% | 100% | 6% | 94% | 100% |
| number | 1 | 18 | 19 | 1 | 16 | 17 |
| 2,500+ | | | | | | |
| percent | 5% | 95% | 100% | — | 100% | 100% |
| number | 1 | 20 | 21 | — | 29 | 29 |
| —2,500 | | | | | | |
| percent | 6% | 94% | 100% | 2% | 98% | 100% |
| number | 3 | 47 | 50 | 1 | 44 | 45 |
| Total | | | | | | |
| percent | 47% | 53% | 100% | 42% | 58% | 100% |
| number | 94 | 107 | 201 | 86 | 120 | 206 |

In observing the legislative party distribution outside New York City, it is seen that there is some Democratic representation in districts of 100,000 or more. However, even these highly urban places produce an appreciably greater proportion of Republicans. It is clear that the partisan breaking point is between the state's single metropolitan center and constituencies of 100,000 plus. All other districts lower down on the urbanization scale are overwhelmingly in the Republican camp.

What is responsible for this sharp drop in Democratic representation outside of New York City? Undoubtedly, the differences which exist between the people who inhabit upstate and mass-city are a major factor. In the latter place there can be found great diversity in the ethnic, racial and religious make-up of the population. Upstate also shows social diversity, but it is not nearly as great as the city's. Here there is emphasis on the values and social character of predominantly Protestant old-stock inhabitants. As analyzed by Lynton K. Caldwell, this is the essence of the matter:

> Outwardly self-confident, the old-stock upstate Yorkers do not ordinarily think of themselves as a "minority group"; yet they sense the insecurity of their social position and their values. There is evident apprehension upstate that in terms of social character—ways of living, thinking, and voting—the old-stock Yorker is in actuality a minority element in the state. . . . Thus tradition, pride, and underlying insecurity induce in upstate New York a sometimes almost paranoid resistance to the sociology and politics of New York City.[19]

But differences in religious, social, and ethnic character do not provide the whole explanation. Ralph Straetz and Frank Munger elaborate upon this:

> Taken as a whole, upstate is far more Republican than

19. Lynton K. Caldwell, *The Government and Administration of New York* (New York: Thomas Y. Crowell Company, 1954), p. 11.

states with similar proportions of urban, industrial, foreign-born, and Catholic population; similarly, upstate cities are more Republican than cities of equivalent size elsewhere in the country. Presumably the difference in partisan attachment lies in the element that distinguishes upstate from the other units, its location within the same state as a metropolitan center that threatens to dominate the state government by sheer force of numbers.[20]

Reference must also be made to legislative malapportionment as another factor which has been responsible for the bipolarization of party representation in the state. Since the representative system was deliberately rigged against the Democrats, they weren't making the extra effort of winning additional seats in other places outside New York City. And because the Republicans, until recently, had been generally assured of majority control in the legislature, they could afford to give less than their best in New York City.

For purposes of political analysis, then, two categories of districts have special relevance: New York City and all other districts. Because Democratic party recruitment depends so heavily upon human resources in the metropolis, its legislative personnel exhibit the traits and behavior patterns of metropolitan politicians. Table 5 shows that they arrive at the legislature comparatively youthful and almost totally inexperienced. As members of what has long been the minority party, they move through the lawmaking chambers at a faster rate than does the opposition.[21] Republicans resemble the relatively rural, small-town politicians which they draw upon. Members of that party are older and evidence a considerable amount of

20. Ralph A. Straetz and Frank J. Munger, *New York Politics* (New York: New York University Press, 1960) , pp. 55–56.

21. In the fifty years prior to 1965, the Republicans have been able to dominate the legislature almost uninterruptedly. During that period, the Democrats were able to win a majority control of both houses on only one occasion.

political experience, particularly in local, elective office. And as they have been the majority, with access to all the key institutional positions, Republicans are inclined toward a longer stay in the legislature.

Table 5. Selected Characteristics of Democratic and Republican Legislators, 1931 and 1951.

| Selected Characteristics | 1931 legislators | | 1951 legislators | |
|---|---|---|---|---|
| | Dem. | Repub. | Dem. | Repub. |
| | (N 94) | (N 107) | (N 86) | (N 120) |
| Age of legislators | | | | |
| —35 years | 42% | 14% | 13% | 7% |
| 36-45 years | 30 | 21 | 49 | 23 |
| 46-55 years | 12 | 27 | 34 | 34 |
| 56-65 years | 14 | 28 | 2 | 23 |
| 66+ years | 2 | 8 | 1 | 9 |
| Unknown | 1 | 2 | 1 | 4 |
| Total | 101% | 100% | 100% | 100% |
| Tenure: no. of years* | | | | |
| 1-4 years | 14% | 14% | 14% | 4% |
| 5-8 years | 30 | 38 | 22 | 12 |
| 9-12 years | 31 | 20 | 18 | 9 |
| 13-16 years | 16 | 17 | 18 | 32 |
| 17+ years | 9 | 11 | 29 | 42 |
| Total | 100% | 100% | 101% | 99% |
| Governmental experience† | | | | |
| None | 87% | 34% | 62% | 38% |
| Local‡ | 7 | 57 | 13 | 52 |
| City | 5 | 10 | 11 | 12 |
| State | 1 | 7 | 9 | 7 |
| National | — | 8 | 16 | 3 |
| Elective§ | 3 | 51 | 5 | 52 |
| Appointive§ | 11 | 27 | 36 | 23 |

* Tenure is accounted for up to the 1966 session.

† Percentages do not total up to 100 percent in this category since a legislator could be counted two or three or four times if he previously held positions on two, three or four levels of government.

‡ This refers to village, town, county and special district government (school-boards).

§ A legislator was counted twice if he previously served in both elective and appointive positions.

## LEGISLATORS AND METROPOLITAN AREAS

It was in 1950 that the United States Bureau of the Census officially recognized the metropolitan area as a new kind of urban phenomenon.[22] This recognition had been slow in coming. Traditionally, attention had always been focused on the compact city as a unit of analysis. But with the coming of the automobile and new and improved methods of home financing and construction, a settlement pattern around the outskirts of most large cities soon became evident. As population and then industry moved outward in growing proportions, the surrounding villages and small cities developed new economic and social attachments to the core cities. After World War II, this transformation became so pronounced that in many areas it was no longer possible to clearly distinguish between urban places and rural places.

By the 1950s, the suburbs in the New York metropolitan region had developed as a new kind of cultural outgrowth with ideas and values often quite different from the large metropolis or the rural countryside. People in these places tend to be preoccupied with PTA meetings, problems of commuting and house valuations. The social ethic prospers here as well as an almost unfaltering belief in grass-roots democracy.

The question now posed is what has been the impact of metropolitan development upon New York representatives. To discern variations, legislators are classified into four categories: central-city Republicans, suburban Republicans, rural Republicans,[23] and Democrats. (Since

22. According to the Bureau of the Census, "standard metropolitan areas" contain at least one city of 50,000 or more population. The area itself is the county or counties containing the core city or cities. Contiguous counties are included in the area if they are densely settled by non-agricultural workers and are social and economically integrated with the core city. United States Bureau of the Census, *Census of Population: 1950,* Vol. I, *Number of Inhabitants,* 1952, pp. xv and xxxiii.

23. In the present sense, the term "rural Republicans" refers to all nonmetropolitan Republicans.

98 percent of all 1951 Democrats were from the central-cities, they were assigned to one inclusive category.) Legislators who served in 1931 were not included in the survey because around cities other than New York, the suburban pattern had not as yet fully emerged; the number of personnel in the suburban grouping would therefore be too small for the derivation of valid conclusions.

Table 6 indicates that suburban legislators are of closer resemblance to their rural colleagues than they are either to central-city Republicans or Democrats. Though younger, they nevertheless show the same extensive background in local, elective office. This is to be expected. According to Robert Wood, the average suburbanite seeks refuge from the anonymity and confusion of the metropolis.[24] As a way of finding roots and a sense of belonging, he strives to resurrect the small community as an autonomous entity and urges participation in its affairs. This can be justified by "our long standing conviction that small political units represent the purest expression of popular rule, that the government closest to home is best."[25] Thus the virtues of small-town government are accorded just as much importance here as in the outlying areas. Suburban politicians, needless to say, subscribe to these values and the abundance of governmental units and offices provides them with sufficient opportunity to realize such goals as part of their own experience.

With reference to tenure, suburban Republicans, like all members of the majority party, manifest many years of legislative service. A significant difference appears, however, when we focus upon duration of county residence. Prior to being elected, only 58 percent of the suburbanites had resided in their respective counties for over 30 years. This is to be compared to about 80 percent of the other lawmakers. Responsible for this is the great flow of popu-

24. Robert C. Wood, *Suburbia, Its People and Their Politics* (Boston: Houghton Mifflin Company, 1959) , Chap. 1.
25. *Ibid.*, p. 12.

Table 6. Selected Characteristics of Rural, Suburban and Central-City Republicans and All Democrats in 1951

| Selected Characteristics | Rural Republicans | Suburban Republicans | Central-City Republicans | All Democrats |
|---|---|---|---|---|
| | (N 59) | (N 26) | (N 35) | (N 86) |
| Age of legislators | | | | |
| —35 yrs. | 5% | 4% | 11% | 13% |
| 36-45 yrs. | 15 | 19 | 40 | 49 |
| 46-55 yrs. | 25 | 46 | 40 | 34 |
| 56-65 yrs. | 36 | 15 | 6 | 2 |
| 66+ yrs. | 14 | 12 | — | 1 |
| Unknown | 5 | 4 | 3 | 1 |
| Total | 100% | 100% | 100% | 100% |
| Tenure: no. of years* | | | | |
| 1-4 yrs. | 2% | 8% | 6% | 14% |
| 5-8 yrs. | 7 | 15 | 14 | 22 |
| 9-12 yrs. | 8 | 8 | 11 | 18 |
| 13-16 yrs. | 34 | 27 | 37 | 18 |
| 17+ yrs. | 49 | 42 | 31 | 29 |
| Total | 100% | 100% | 99% | 101% |
| Government experience† | | | | |
| None | 31% | 31% | 54% | 62% |
| Local‡ | 59 | 65 | 31 | 13 |
| City | 10 | 4 | 20 | 11 |
| State | 9 | — | 9 | 9 |
| National | 5 | 4 | — | 16 |
| Elective§ | 59 | 54 | 37 | 5 |
| Appointive§ | 24 | 27 | 17 | 36 |
| Duration of county residence# | | | | |
| 1-10 yrs. | —% | —% | —% | —% |
| 11-20 yrs. | 14 | 12 | 9 | 6 |
| 21-30 yrs. | 7 | 23 | 11 | 13 |
| 31+ yrs. | 80 | 58 | 80 | 79 |
| Unknown | — | 8 | — | 2 |
| Total | 101% | 101% | 100% | 100% |

Note: All Democrats are considered the equivalent of all central-city Democrats.

* Tenure is accounted for up to the 1966 session.

† Percentages here do not total up to 100 percent. In computing percentages, a legislator could be counted two or three or four times if he

lation into the urban fringe areas. Accordingly, it is quite possible that these migrants may be changing the very recruitment base of the Republican party—a matter of future investigation.

## SUMMATION—BACKGROUND PROFILES

This chapter has highlighted the fact that where districts vary, representatives will vary as well. The legislator-politician is, after all, a human being who is influenced by the social and political environment from which he is derived. Thus, the lawmakers from the more urban constituencies tend to be younger and very much the political novices. To them, legislative office is usually a first step in their careers and they don't hold to this position quite as long as do those from the rural districts. The relatively rural legislators tend to be older and show more experience in public office. Having achieved a seat in the legislature, they are inclined to hold on to it for a longer period of time.

The most pronounced contrasts in legislator characteristics seem to exist between the New York City districts and all others; and the party affiliations of the lawmakers reflect this. New York City is overwhelmingly represented by Democrats. Outside the metropolis, it is the Republicans who predominate. Accordingly, each party is committed to the recruitment of a different kind of "political animal," affected by two broadly different milieus. The average Democrat is very much the New York City politician: he is youthful, politically inexperienced, and moves through the legislature at a relatively rapid pace. Where

previously held positions on two, three or four levels of government, i.e., local, city, state, national.

‡ This refers to village, town, county and special district government (school boards).

§ A legislator was counted twice if he previously served in both elective and appointive positions.

# Duration of county residence prior to election to the legislature.

he does indicate previous experience in government, it is more often due to appointment rather than election. The average Republican has traditionally come from a more rural society. Consequently he is older, shows a more extensive political background—particularly in local elective office—and acquires longer tenure in the legislature. Because of these differences, moreover, it can be assumed that the members of the two parties continue to play out different roles in the political system, something which will be investigated shortly.

In assessing the impact of metropolitan development on New York legislators, it was found that representatives from the central-city, whether Republican or Democratic, tend to be younger and politically inexperienced. As might be expected, the variable of urbanism appears to be more pertinent than party affiliation. Central-city Republicans, however, show much more elective office experience and tend to achieve greater tenure once they are elected to the legislature. For the most part, this is because such persons come from central-cities which are of smaller scale than New York City. But more significant is the fact that the growth of the suburbs may be changing the very recruitment base of the Republican party. Suburban Republicans are relative newcomers to their area of residence and consequently they manifest attributes which diverge from the traditional Republican norms.

# 3

# PATTERNS OF SOCIAL AND ETHNIC RECRUITMENT

Perhaps more than in any other state in the union, New York has been exposed to what Samuel Lubell has labeled "League of Nations politics."[1] By this it is meant that political issues and campaigns in the state tend to revolve around the competing claims and strivings of the various racial, religious, and ethnic groups who live there. It follows, then, that if we are to understand the behavior patterns of legislators, we must see them as members of these different groupings.

New York has long been the port of entry for those coming from foreign countries. Historians relate how, after the American Revolution, successive waves of immigrants found their way into the state, usually for the purpose of finding a better place in which to live and work.[2] At first, in the 1820s, it was the New England Yankees who came and who carried with them their Puritan beliefs. At about the same time Englishmen, Frenchmen and Germans were arriving from foreign shores to try their luck in the New World. Since these groups were very similar to those which had settled earlier, social ad-

---

1. Samuel Lubell, *The Ruture of American Politics* (New York: Doubleday and Company, 1956), p. 79.

2. For a good general treatment of this matter, see Oscar Handlin, *The Newcomers* (Cambridge, Mass.: Harvard University Press, 1959).

justments were not too difficult and there was little friction between the old and new.

The story is quite a different one after 1840. At this later time, immigrants were arriving whose manners and beliefs appeared too alien to the settled natives. This was true of the Irish Catholics who were fleeing the famines and deprivations of their home country. This was also true of the Italian Catholics and the East European Jews who were arriving in ever larger numbers after 1880.

Toward the end of the nineteenth century, the descendants of the original settlers identified themselves as Anglo-Saxons, a term which aptly served to set them apart from those of new immigrant stock. The basic characteristic of this group was its Protestantism and it included not only the old English and Dutch families but also the Scots, English, Welsh and even the German and Frenchmen who came later and affiliated themselves with it.

As for the immigrants and their descendants who could not readily assimilate, ethnic affiliations have remained important to the third generation and beyond. Oscar Handlin writes that:

> . . . ethnicity is a permanent quality of the American society, particularly in cities. The expectations of half a century ago that a melting-pot process would ultimately fuse the American population into a single homogeneous product have not been realized. Instead, although immigration has ended and today's Jews, Italians and Irish are far different from their European parents and grandparents, groups derived from the original experience of immigration have persisted. Indeed, the events of the past thirty years have actually stimulated the tendency to adhere to such clusters and have renewed their vitality.[3]

3. *The New York Times*, September 22, 1963, Section 7, p. 3. See, also, Nathan Glazer and Daniel P. Moynihan, *Beyond the Melting Pot: The Negroes, Puerto Ricans, Jews, Italians and Irish of New York City* (Cambridge, Mass.: The M.I.T. Press and Harvard University Press, 1963) .

The flow of large numbers of Negroes and Puerto Ricans into New York toward the middle of the twentieth century represented the latest phase of the state's immigration history. These people have had less difficulty than the others in maintaining a sense of group identification —the color of their skin serves as a continual reminder.

## SOCIAL MOBILITY

In most cases, particularly after the 1840s, the newcomers were coming poor and destitute; and lacking skills, they usually took the lowliest, most menial jobs. Thus, one problem that almost all immigrant groups have had to face is how to move out of the lowest ranks of society. Among the limited possibilities, an important alternative has been to enter politics; for here, the ability to depend upon an ethnic following is an undeniable asset.

The social origins of New York legislators, as indicated by their fathers' occupations, gives some measure of such striving. In Table 9, we see that a large proportion of lawmakers started life in the lower echelons of society where the bread-winner of the family was a salaried worker or an industrial wage-earner. There were many instances, also (only partially revealed by our statistics), where the family members cooperated in operating a small-business establishment; the corner grocery, the candy store, and the tavern are typical examples. From out of such beginnings a goodly number of our subjects subsequently managed to achieve upward social mobility.[4]

---

4. An unavoidable limitation to the data collected in Table 9 is that in about 20 percent of the cases no information on fathers' occupational class could be found. Consequently, it must be recognized that our determinations will not be conclusive but must serve merely as a rough indicator. In a few selected instances, where the father's occupation was not known, other criteria were used to assess initial class status. For example, biographical descriptions of youthful poverty or of a legislator working his way through school.

This seems to fit the general thesis that politicians use their profession as a means of climbing the class ladder.

Table 9. Social Origins: Occupational Class of Fathers Compared With Legislative Sons, Classified by Political Party.

| Occupational class | Democrats | | Republicans | | All legislators | |
|---|---|---|---|---|---|---|
| | fathers | sons | fathers | sons | fathers | sons |
| **1931 legislators** | | | | | | |
| Professional | 6% | 67% | 15% | 39% | 11% | 52% |
| Executives, proprietors, and officials | 9 | 6 | 13 | 23 | 11 | 15 |
| Minor professional, small businessmen & technical | 17 | 17 | 13 | 15 | 15 | 16 |
| Farmers | 2 | 1 | 27 | 20 | 15 | 11 |
| Clerical, sales and kindred workers | 8 | 6 | 4 | 1 | 6 | 4 |
| Skilled, semi-skilled & unskilled workers | 34 | 2 | 11 | 2 | 22 | 2 |
| Unknown | 24 | — | 17 | — | 20 | — |
| Total percent | 100% | 99% | 100% | 100% | 100% | 100% |
| **1951 legislators** | | | | | | |
| Professional | 14% | 79% | 15% | 48% | 15% | 61% |
| Executives, proprietors and officials | 5 | 6 | 11 | 20 | 8 | 14 |
| Minor professional, small businessmen & technical | 20 | 8 | 19 | 20 | 19 | 15 |
| Farmers | — | — | 17 | 8 | 10 | 4 |
| Clerical, sales and kindred workers | 5 | 5 | 3 | 2 | 3 | 3 |
| Skilled, semi-skilled & unskilled workers | 35 | 2 | 15 | 2 | 23 | 2 |
| Unknown | 22 | — | 20 | — | 21 | — |
| Total percent | 101% | 100% | 100% | 100% | 99% | 99% |

To quote from Edward A. Shils: "In the United States politicians have an unusually high degree of social mobility. Politicians, more than any other profession, represent

the realization of the idea of the poor boy who takes advantage of the opportunities of an open society and rises to
the top. Even more than businessmen and intellectuals,
American politicians have moved from the society of their
birth and youth."[5]

If we compare our two sample sessions as to mobility
patterns, some differences are noticeable. The major
change is that more of the 1951 lawmakers reflect middle-
class beginnings. Increases can be noted among those
whose fathers were professional and small businessmen.
Decreases have occurred among those who are derived
from executive-proprietor and farm families. Stated in another way, more 1951 legislators have been reared in
households where the father worked as a lawyer, ac-
countant, or small merchant rather than as a banker, in-
dustrialist, or farmer. It is quite possible that as the Federal government has come to assume a more active role
in American society, upper-class elements find greater
incentive for service on that level;[6] as a consequence,
upward-striving middle-class persons probably have better
access to state government than was previously the case.
The decrease of farmers, furthermore, is largely a manifestation of spreading urbanism.

Of additional significance are the contrasts which can
be discerned in the social origins of Republicans and
Democrats. Both in 1931 and 1951, the fathers of Republicans are found predominantly in the upper levels of the
class hierarchy while the largest proportion of Democrats
are from the lowest stratum. More than one observer who
was interviewed characterized New York Democrats as
"men on the make." The data lend support to this observation: the Democratic members of the lawmaking

5. Edward A. Shils, "The Legislator and His Environment," *University
of Chicago Law Review*, 18 (Spring, 1951) : 581.
6. This idea is suggested by the findings in Donald Matthews' study of
American Presidents, Vice Presidents, Cabinet members, Senators, Representatives, Governors and state legislators. See *The Social Background of
Political Decision-Makers* (New York: Random House, 1954), pp. 23-30.

body evidence much more upward mobility than those who are affiliated with the opposing party; and more often than not, as we shall see, it is the combination of the professions of law and politics which makes this possible. (This theme is developed in Chapter 7.)

## ETHNIC RECRUITMENT

During political campaigns, the party organizations make their appeal directly to the different interests, factions and groups of the community. When successfully done, it helps win elections. In polyglot New York, party strategies tend to emphasize the distinctive qualities of the various ethnic, religious and racial blocs. For example, great stress is placed on the ethnically "balanced" ticket. Partly as a result of this, ethnic identity is one of the potent ingredients of the state's politics and there is usually keen awareness of "who gets what."

It is with this in mind that we examine the manner in which ethnic groups have been accepted into the New York legislature. Although there are many such groups in New York, we shall consider only those which are numerically most important. These are: (1) "Old Stock": individuals who are of third-generation American families and who display no other ethnic characteristics. Combined with this group are those of British birth; (2) Irish: individuals who were born in Ireland or whose parents or grandparents were born there and who display some identifiable Irish characteristics; (3) Italian: persons who were born in Italy or whose parents or grandparents were born there and who show some identifiable Italian characteristics; (4) German: the same criteria as for the Irish and Italians; (5) Jewish: persons who were born Jews and who display some clear Jewish identification; (6) Negro. In addition, we take note of such related characteristics as religious affiliation and immigrant status.

Table 10 provides us with a picture of the contrasting recruitment roles performed by the two political parties. Dominating the Republican legislators are the "Old Stock" Protestant Americans or Yankees as they are often referred to. As far back as the 1830s and 40s, "upper class" elements began to leave the Democratic party as Tammany Hall undertook a "systematic gathering in of the naturalized citizens. . . ."[7] Indeed, the Whig opposition, forerunners to modern Republicanism, soon became a refuge for many rebelling nativists. Dixon Ryan Fox illustrates the attitude of such persons by recording the following conversation:

"Why, what singular notions you have, Mr. ——!" exclaimed the lady; "I hope you are not advocate of the rabble?"

"Certainly not; I represent the people in my township."

"You do not understand me. When I speak of the 'rabble,' I mean those who have no interest in our institutions,— foreign paupers and adventurers, and particularly the Irish. I have no objection to liberty in the abstract. I think all men, with the exception of our negroes, ought to be free; but I cannot bear the ridiculous notions of equality which seem to take hold of our people. . . ."

"I have always been a democrat."

"Oh! You are a dem-o-crat, are you?"[8]

If the Yankee Republican hegemony managed to persist through the 1930s, there is evidence that it has been decidedly attentuated since. Between 1931 and 1951, our statistics show a sizable decrease of such types in the Republican legislative ranks as individuals of other backgrounds have begun to find their way in. Not only have more Irish, Jews and Italians been accepted, but almost

7. Gustavius Myers, *The History of Tammany Hall* (New York: Boni and Liveright, 1917) , p. 129.

8. Dixon Ryan Fox, *The Decline of Aristocracy in the Politics of New York* (New York: Columbia University Press, 1919) , p. 375.

all those of German origin appear to have switched their allegiances to the Republican party.[9]

Table 10. Demographic Characteristics of 1931 and 1951 New York Legislators, Classified by Political Party.

| Characteristics | 1931 Legislators | | | 1951 Legislators | | |
|---|---|---|---|---|---|---|
| | Dem. | Repub. | All | Dem. | Repub. | All |
| **Immigrant status** | | | | | | |
| Foreign born | 6% | 3% | 5% | 14% | 7% | 10% |
| Second generation | 37 | 7 | 21 | 33 | 13 | 21 |
| Total percent | 43% | 10% | 26% | 47% | 20% | 31% |
| **Ethnic status** | | | | | | |
| "Old Stock" | 6% | 87% | 50% | 3% | 65% | 39% |
| Irish | 48 | 2 | 23 | 33 | 7 | 17 |
| Jews | 25 | 2 | 12 | 33 | 3 | 16 |
| Italians | 2 | 2 | 2 | 17 | 6 | 11 |
| Negroes | 1 | — | 1 | 5 | — | 2 |
| Germans* | 5 | 1 | 3 | 1 | 10 | 6 |
| Others | 6 | — | 3 | 2 | 2 | 2 |
| Unknown | 6 | 6 | 6 | 6 | 7 | 7 |
| Total percent | 99% | 100% | 100% | 100% | 100% | 100% |
| **Religion** | | | | | | |
| Protestant | 12% | 86% | 51% | 9% | 63% | 40% |
| Catholic | 62 | 6 | 32 | 53 | 27 | 38 |
| Jewish | 25 | 2 | 12 | 33 | 3 | 16 |
| Unknown | 2 | 6 | 5 | 5 | 7 | 6 |
| Total percent | 101% | 100% | 100% | 100% | 100% | 100% |

*Does not include Jews of German origin.

It is the ethnic minorities who predominate within the Democratic organization. Undoubtedly, the greater amenability of this party to the newcomer can be attributed

9. Samuel Lubell suggests that German Americans were to some extent alienated from the Democrats because of the party's leadership role during the conflict with Germany in World War II, *The Future of American Politics,* pp. 143–59. Probably a more pertinent reason in New York is that they could no longer identify with the mass of newcomers who continued to flow into the Democratic party.

largely to the fact that it draws its strength from the state's massive urban center, New York City. In 1950, more than 56 percent of the city's population was classified as being either foreign born or of foreign parentage; and formerly, in 1930, some 73 percent of the city's population was so characterized. Ed Flynn, the man who ruled the Bronx Democratic party for more than twenty-five years, comments on the significance of immigration to his party:

> During the latter half of the nineteenth century, immigrants were pouring into America through the Port of New York. Many remained there, the majority settling in Manhattan. It was inevitable that they should play a decisive role in New York politics. But the so-called "better element" would have none of them. The young Republican party in New York reflected this attitude. The immigrants, on the other hand, being human, wanted friends, jobs, the chance to become citizens. Tammany was smart enough to offer them all three, in return for lifetime and often second-, third-, and fourth-generation fealty to the party. It was as simple and as obvious as that.[10]

In the early 1930s, it was the Irish who controlled New York Democratic politics. The first of the ethnics to have come to power, their political grip was still holding strong. Less influential but also well entrenched were the Jews. Such others as the Italians and Negroes were barely represented among the personnel of governmental institutions. All of this is quite apparent in viewing the 1931 legislature. The basic problem of the latter two groups, then, was how to gain entrance. Daniel Bell describes this with reference to the Italians:

> The Italian community in New York has for years nursed a grievance against the Irish and, to a lesser extent, the Jewish political groups for monopolizing political power. They

10. Edward J. Flynn, *You're the Boss* (New York: The Viking Press, 1947), pp. 10–11.

complained about the lack of judicial jobs, and the small number—usually one—of Italian congressmen, the lack of representation on the state tickets. But the Italians lacked the means to make their ambition a reality. Although they formed a large voting bloc, there was rarely sufficient wealth to finance political clubs. Italian immigrants, largely poor peasants from southern Italy and Sicily, lacked the mercantile experience of the Jews and the political experience gained in the seventy-five-year history of Irish immigration.[11]

By the 1950s, the Italians had apparently acquired the kind of resources which would promote their political advancement. This is indicated by a 15 percent increase of Italians within the Democratic party. Jews have also fared well and by 1951 they had caught up with the descending Irish. Ironically, the groups which show the lowest proportion of Democratic personnel are the "Old Stock" Americans and the Negroes. The native Americans, however, manifest substantial influence in the opposition party. The Negroes, in 1951, had not yet achieved full political recognition within any of the partisan organizations.

## CLASS STATUS

According to our data, most of those who participate in New York politics achieve worldly success. Not only do legislator-politicians rise beyond their fathers as previously noted, but, when compared to the general population most of them are found on the top rungs of the socio-economic ladder. In Table 11 we see that 84 percent of the 1931 lawmakers were located in the professional or executive-proprietor categories; in 1951, the percentage was 91. Among New Yorkers generally, only about 20 percent were similarly classified for the years

---

11. Daniel Bell, *The End of Ideology* (New York: Collier Books, 1962), p. 144.

1940 and 1950.[12] At the same time, skilled, semiskilled and unskilled workers are rarely found in the lawmaking body. If the New Deal "revolution" was supposed to have provided new and improved opportunity to the laboring interests of society, there is no visible evidence of this in the New York legislature: the proportion of wage earners and low-salaried workers is no greater after the New Deal years than before it.

To what may we attribute this? At least partly responsible are the limitations imposed upon working-class persons by the very nature of their occupations. It is usually the case that they have little opportunity during the normal work day to engage in activities which are necessary to a successful career, e.g., campaigning, doing favors for others. On the other hand, people in the professions and in business will often boost their occupational careers when they achieve legislative office. A lawyer, for example, can count on making new business connections. This is one reason why so many are drawn to the legislature.

Another factor which explains the dearth of working-class persons is that they usually do not have the advantage of a good education. As can be seen in our table, members of the legislature are of considerably higher educational accomplishment than is the population of the state. This corresponds with the findings of a number of other studies which show that political activity and interest increase with higher educational achievement.[13] In addition, certain important political skills such as verbal ability, proficiency as a concilator or manipulator, are generally lost to the poorly educated.

12. The occupational classification system used in the 1930 Census and earlier censuses were markedly different from the later system. Thus, the earliest usable statistics for New York State are derived from the census reports of 1940.

13. J. L. Woodward and E. Roper, "Political Activity of American Citizens," *The American Political Science Review*, 44 (December, 1950): 872–85. See also John M. Foskett, "Social Structure and Social Participation," *The American Sociological Review*, 20 (August, 1955): 431–38.

Table 11. Class Status as Measured by Occupation and Education: New York Legislators Compared to New York's Population.

| Class indicators | 1931 legislators | N.Y. pop.* 1940 | 1951 legislators | N.Y. pop. 1950 |
|---|---|---|---|---|
| **Occupational class** | | | | |
| Professional & technical | 56% | 10% | 64% | 11% |
| Executives, proprietors and officials | 28 | 10 | 27 | 11 |
| Farmers | 11 | 2 | 4 | 2 |
| Clerical, sales & kindred workers | 3 | 23 | 3 | 24 |
| Skilled, semiskilled, & unskilled workers | 2 | 54 | 2 | 52 |
| Occupations not reported | — | 1 | — | 1 |
| Total percent | 100% | 100% | 100% | 101% |
| **Educational level†** | | | | |
| No schooling | —% | 6% | —% | 4% |
| Grade school | 14 | 54 | 3 | 41 |
| High school | 20 | 28 | 19 | 38 |
| College or professional school | 63 | 10 | 76 | 13 |
| Unknown | 3 | 2 | 2 | 4 |
| Total percent | 100% | 100% | 100% | 100% |

SOURCE: United States Bureau of the Census, *Census of population: 1950,* Vol. II, Part 32, pp. 63, 68.

*Census statistics on occupation and education during the period prior to 1940 were either classified differently or were not available.

†Level of education for New York's population is estimated for all those 25 years old and over.

Given the fact that a large proportion of legislators are employed as lawyers—46 percent in 1931, 55 percent in 1951—the insights of Max Weber are quite relevant here. The noted German sociologist explains: "Neither the worker nor . . . the entrepreneur, especially the modern, large scale entrepreneur" is readily available as a politician. For they must spend most, if not all of their available time, "in the service of economic acquisition." "For purely organizational reasons, it is easier for the lawyer to be dispensible; and therefore the lawyer has played an incomparably greater, and often even a dominant role as a professional politician."[14]

At this point we raise a related question: Is it the case that most mobile legislators deliberately adopt law as the profession best calculated to contribute to a career in politics? We pursue this matter in Chapter 7.

*Class and parties*

If we refer to Table 9, it can be seen that the Republican party has been undergoing some transformation between the years 1931 and 1951. Where the businessman, executive, and farmer formerly dominated the party, the middle groupings of society have since entered its ranks in larger numbers; in 1951, it is the professionals and small businessmen who predominate more than ever.

In part, this is the result of the growing availability of middle-class persons, an availability that comes with the suburbanization of rural areas. Professional and technical workers have been moving out to what was formerly the countryside; and the spread of service trades in the urban fringe areas has introduced greater numbers of small businessmen.[15] These newcomers, in turn, have served to drastically reduce the proportion of farmers. Legislators are very much part of this transition, particularly the Republicans who dominate in suburban and rural areas.

Upon viewing the Democrats, we see that they have drawn an extremely large proportion of their members

---

14. Max Weber in H. H. Gerth and C. Wright Mills, eds., *From Max Weber* (New York: Oxford University Press, 1946), p. 85.

15. Edgar M. Hoover and Raymond Vernon present a detailed analysis of such changes in the New York Metropolitan Region in their book *Anatomy of a Metropolis* (Cambridge, Mass.: Harvard University Press, 1959).

from among the professionals. Those who are so employed have increased from 67 percent in 1931 to 79 percent in 1951, well above what the Republicans show. At the same time, it should be noted that most of the other occupational-class groupings within the party show a percentage drop. Especially significant is the fact that the vast majority of Democratic professionals are lawyers. Apparently, there is something peculiar to the political life of a large urban complex like New York City—the home of the Democrats—which favors the legal practitioner. At this time, however, it would interest us to inquire into the following: if there is a higher proportion of lawyers among the Democrats, does this mean that the members of this party are on a higher class level than the Republicans?

### Republican and Democratic lawyers

Most members of the legal profession partake in a style of living which clearly sets them apart from those of other occupations. Yet we find different status gradations within the profession. Obviously an experienced corporation lawyer is a man of higher standing than the young barrister who must seek out a living by "hustling." Thus, it is not enough to merely count lawyers in making distinctions between Democrats and Republicans. We must also try to assess differences in quality.

One way of effecting this, though it is by no means definitive, is to investigate the kinds of law schools which the lawyer-legislators attended. On the basis of two studies which were undertaken by Alfred Z. Reed in the 1920s, it is possible to distinguish four types of law schools.[16] These are: (1) Full-time law schools with high entrance requirements which are part of well-established colleges or universities; (2) Low entrance schools which offer full-

16. *Training For the Public Profession of Law* (New York: Carnegie Foundation for the Advancement of Teaching, 1921), Bulletin #15. Also *Present-Day Law Schools* (New York: Carnegie Foundation for the Advancement of Teaching, 1928), Bulletin #21.

time courses of standard length; (3) Low entrance schools in which student attendance is mostly part-time and where classroom exercise is most often scheduled for the evening; (4) Short-course law schools which are geared principally to the purpose of helping students pass the state bar examination.

As judged from the data in Table 12, it appears that many more Democrats have attended the kind of law school where training time is sacrificed to permit self-supporting employment. In comparison, Republicans show a substantially greater percentage of members going to the best law schools.

Table 12. Types of Law Schools Attended by 1931 and 1951 New York Legislators, Classified by Political Party.

| Types of Law Schools | 1931 legislators | | | 1951 legislators | | |
|---|---|---|---|---|---|---|
| | Dems. | Repus. | All | Dem. | Repus. | All |
| High entrance, full-time | 2% | 32% | 14% | 11% | 25% | 17% |
| Low entrance, full-time | 4 | 40 | 18 | 5 | 46 | 22 |
| Low entrance, part-time | 89 | 10 | 57 | 85 | 23 | 58 |
| Short course and non-attendance* | 5 | 18 | 11 | — | 6 | 3 |
| Total percent | 100% | 100% | 100% | 101% | 100% | 100% |
| Total number | 55 | 38 | 93 | 65 | 48 | 113 |

*Non-attendance refers to a situation where the lawyer did not go to school but passed his bar examination through means of correspondence courses and/or guidance of established lawyers.

From all indications, then, Republican lawmakers—lawyers and others—are of higher socio-economic status than Democrats. In light of some observations made by V. O. Key in his investigations, this finding bears significance. Consider the following:

Outside the South, the Republican group has far greater resources for the support of leadership as well as a far larger reservoir of persons with leadership skills on which to draw.

Well-connected lawyers, businessmen with time and money to devote to politics, and, perhaps to a lesser extent, persons with skill in professional politics gravitate in greater degree to the Republican party than to the Democratic. By the secondary network of economic relations within their own group—legal retainers, insurance commissions, real estate transactions, and the like—the business community within the Republican party can sustain a class whose time and energies may be dedicated principally to the practice of politics.

The Democratic party, on the other hand, enjoys the handicaps in recruiting leadership created by its position as a party devoted in principle to mass causes. By and large it must depend upon somewhat different classes of individuals to man its leadership echelons.[17]

## SUMMARY AND CONCLUSION: THE CIRCULATION OF ETHNIC ELITES

In his *The Future of American Politics,* Samuel Lubell asserts: "As its large families have grown to voting age and as it has developed its own leadership, each minority group has been demanding an ever-increasing share of political recognition."[18] Within the legislative chambers of New York, a pattern can be discerned in the way these groups have come to achieve such recognition while at the same time intruding upon and even replacing other groups that had been dominant.

In the 1930s, the Republicans were heavily oriented toward persons of old-stock Yankee background who could be expected to reflect ideas and values which would not conflict with the party's basic ideological premises. As described by Richard Hofstadter, the underlying political ethic here

17. V. O. Key, *American State Politics: An Introduction* (New York: Alfred A. Knopf, 1956), pp. 256–57.
18. P. 70.

assumed and demanded the constant, disinterested activity of the citizen in public affairs, argued that political life ought to be run, to a greater degree than it was, in accordance with general principles and abstract laws apart from and superior to personal needs, and expressed a common feeling that government should be in good part an effort to moralize the lives of individuals while economic life should be intimately related to the stimulation and development of individual character.[19]

Thus Republican preoccupation with the "right type" of persons has served to exclude immigrant-based peoples as a threat; for the political ethic of such types has been quite different:

The other system, founded upon the European backgrounds of the immigrants, upon their unfamiliarity with independent political action, their familiarity with hierarchy and authority, and upon the urgent needs that so often grew out of their migration, took for granted that the political life of the individual would arise out of family needs, interpreted political and civic relations chiefly in terms of personal obligations, and placed strong personal loyalties above allegiance to abstract codes of laws and morals.[20]

It wasn't until the Irish, Jews, and Italians could acquire economic and social "respectability" that Republican restrictions slowly loosened. It is interesting to note, however, that these minorities were accepted into the party only after they had found a place for themselves within the Democratic organization. It is the Democrats that have performed the function of recruiting and assimilating the newcomer into politics, and into society for that matter.

But even within the Democratic party there is evidence

---

19. *The Age of Reform* (New York: Alfred A. Knopf, 1955) , p. 9.
20. *Ibid.*

of a continuing struggle between newer ethnic groups that make their claim to representation and older entrenched blocs that have been reluctant to permit such recognition. The Irish were very slow to make room for the Jews and both of these managed to keep a tight squeeze on the Italians. The political achievements of still newer groups like the Negroes and Puerto Ricans have been minimal. Thus it can be seen that new minorities do not gain entrance to places of power until long after they have grown to considerable size in the electorate. Yet, in spite of such social lag, history illustrates the vulnerability of the party organization to numbers. Negro spokesmen are probably anticipating the full effects of this principle when they periodically demand that members of their race should get a percentage of legislative and other positions which is commensurate with the percentage of enrolled Negro voters.

# 4

# THE PROBLEM OF CONFLICTS
# OF INTEREST

The Madisonian view of contending factional interests invariably pursuing their separate goals in the polity is fundamental to an understanding of the legislative process. For in the fulfillment of their representative role, legislators are expected to give voice to the needs and desires of the varied geographical and functional groupings of society.

But while society condones a "conflict of interests" as a natural consequence of the representative function, there is no such endorsement for "conflicts of interest." The latter refers to situations in which an official's conduct of his office conflicts with his private interests.[1] Herein lies the problem of almost all public bodies: namely, at what point in the course of deciding public policy is the office-holder acting primarily in behalf of his own needs to the detriment of the common good? At what point is he no longer the representative but the self-seeker? Needless to say there are no hard and fast answers to such questions. What makes the matter even more complicated is that as

1. This is the definition provided by Robert S. Getz, *Congressional Ethics: The Conflict of Interest Issue* (Princeton, New Jersey: D. Van Nostrand Company, 1966), pp. 3–4. See also the Association of the Bar of the City of New York, *Conflict of Interest and Federal Service* (Cambridge, Mass.: Harvard University Press, 1960), p. 3.

government has come to assume a greater responsibility in the affairs of the community, a clear separation of the purely public from the purely private is no longer possible. In the legislature, almost any bill at any time involves the vested stakes of at least some groups. Lawmakers are themselves members of many different organizations which stand to gain or lose on the basis of legislative proposals. In addition, such persons have occupational and financial interests which are affected, sometimes substantially, by the very laws they help to enact.

The purpose of the present chapter is to make some assessment of this situation in the New York legislature. In addition we ask: What are the special ethical problems? Is there any way of resolving some of the underlying ambiguities?

## THE ORGANIZATIONAL LIFE OF LEGISLATORS

A first step is to consider the extent and nature of the lawmakers' organizational attachments. Where such affiliations are extensive, we might expect that the potential for conflicts-of-interest would be substantial. And by looking at the kinds of groups that the legislators belong to, we can begin to comprehend the nature of their support as well as their interest biases.

Table 13 indicates that legislators are joiners; that is, most of them were members of five or more organizations in the course of their political careers. What we have here, then, is a pattern of group affiliations which is considerably more extensive than anything ever reported for the general population. Using returns from national sample surveys, for example, Charles Wright and Herbert Hyman found that fewer than four percent of the respondents belonged to four or more organized groups.[2]

---

2. "Voluntary Association Memberships of American Adults: Evidence from National Sample Surveys," *The American Sociological Review* 23 (June, 1958) : 284–94.

Table 13. Profile of Organizational Life for 1931 and 1951 Legislators: Number and Kind of Affiliations as well as Leadership.

| | 1931 legislators | | | 1951 legislators | | |
|---|---|---|---|---|---|---|
| | Dem. | Repub. | All | Dem. | Repub. | All |
| **Number of organizations*** | | | | | | |
| 1 to 4 | 43% | 38% | 40% | 22% | 33% | 29% |
| 5 to 8 | 48 | 47 | 47 | 45 | 43 | 44 |
| 9 to 12 | 8 | 14 | 11 | 26 | 18 | 21 |
| 13 plus | 1 | 1 | 1 | 7 | 5 | 6 |
| Total | 100% | 100% | 99% | 100% | 99% | 100% |
| **Types of organizations** | | | | | | |
| Business & property | 13% | 22% | 18% | 10% | 27% | 17% |
| Labor | 5 | 1 | 3 | 5 | 3 | 4 |
| Farm | 1 | 24 | 13 | 1 | 19 | 12 |
| Ethnic &/or religious | 46 | 16 | 30 | 69 | 30 | 46 |
| Social & fraternal | 61 | 78 | 70 | 62 | 73 | 69 |
| Professional | 22 | 23 | 23 | 57 | 25 | 38 |
| Veterans | 20 | 18 | 19 | 35 | 23 | 28 |
| Civic & Community | 11 | 22 | 16 | 30 | 28 | 29 |
| Other | 2 | 5 | 3 | — | 10 | 5 |
| **Leadership in organizations†** | | | | | | |
| Business & property | 4% | 7% | 6% | 5% | 11% | 8% |
| Labor | 3 | — | 2 | — | 3 | 2 |
| Farm | 1 | 21 | 10 | — | 11 | 6 |
| Ethnic &/or religious | 11 | 8 | 9 | 23 | 8 | 14 |
| Social & fraternal | 5 | 22 | 14 | 12 | 22 | 18 |
| Professional | 1 | 6 | 4 | 9 | 11 | 10 |
| Veterans | 3 | 3 | 3 | 6 | 4 | 5 |
| Civic & Community | 9 | 15 | 10 | 17 | 12 | 15 |
| Other | 1 | 3 | 2 | — | 8 | 4 |

* Church affiliation counts as membership in one organization.
† The criteria for leadership is service as either an officer, director or trustee in an organization.

Why do legislators belong to so many groups? There are at least a few probable reasons. First, numerous studies have shown that there is an increase in the number of

formal affiliations the higher the class status of individuals.[3] As was previously discerned, lawmakers are generally of high social status. Moreover, they evidence high
social mobility; that is, they indicate an ability to rise
from low to higher social standing which also serves to in-
duce a more active involvement in associations.

In addition, and this is perhaps most important, legislators are constantly faced with the task of rallying support at the polls. This often includes party primary
elections as well as the regular interparty elections. Consequently, legislative candidates deliberately join organizations for the purpose of making friends and getting
known. On the other hand, political interest groups generally have an important stake in the kind of men who
occupy public office. The candidate whose background
and platform best meet the needs and goals of a particular organization can usually count on the group to back
him in his political endeavors. Hence, there is a natural
attraction between formal groups and politicians—they
search for one another for purposes of mutual accom-
modation.[4]

Not only are legislators joiners, but according to our
data, a larger proportion of them belonged to more organizations in 1951 than was previously the case. We can
assume that this is not only a reflection of their improved
economic status, but that the changing political system
has come to require the greater social involvement of those
who participate in politics.

## Affiliations of Democrats and Republicans

In comparing the organization affiliations of party per-

3. For example, Mirra Komarovsky, "The Voluntary Associations of
Urban Dwellers," *The American Sociological Review* 11 (December,
1946): 698; W. Lloyd Warner and Paul S. Lunt, *The Social Life of a
Modern Community* (New Haven, Conn.: Yale University Press, 1941),
p. 303.

4. Belle Zeller presents a useful description of this as it pertains to
New York legislators. See *Pressure Politics in New York* (New York:
Prentice-Hall, 1937), pp. 237–40.

sonnel, some interesting contrasts appear. Most outstanding is the large percentage of Democrats who are affiliated with ethnic and religious associations. In light of the fact that members of this party are derived almost entirely from immigrant peoples, this finding should not be too surprising. For church and ethnic associations are the means by which they have been able to hold on to old friendships and maintain a sense of group identity.

But what is noteworthy is the fact that Democratic legislators have increased their ties to such organizations considerably between 1931 and 1951 (46–69 percent). This would seem to contradict the popular idea of an eventual assimilation and absorption of foreign-stock people into an homogeneous American population. To the contrary, the growth of ethnic memberships can be seen as a strengthening of ethnic bonds.[5] Democratic politicians, furthermore, who rely on the ethnic label for electoral backing, understandably seek such associations and strive to maintain them—all the more so as the distinctive signs of language and custom begin to disappear.

Since Republicans are predominantly old-stock Protestant, ethnic organizations are largely superfluous to them. Their social needs are better satisfied through their lodges and fraternal associations. Even their farm organizations like the Grange serve a social as well as an economic function.[6] Over the years, however, as the Irish, Italians, and Jews have gradually penetrated the ranks of the Republican party,[7] there is clearly an increase in Republican ties to ethnic and religious groups. Thus it is seen that as the social base of a political party changes, so too does the potential influence of certain kinds of organizations.

5. This lends support to Glazer and Moynihan's thesis in their book *Beyond the Melting Pot.*
6. For an intriguing discussion of the organizational life of an upstate New York village, see Arthur Vidich and Joseph Bensman, pp. 23–29.
7. See Table 10.

In surveying economic affiliations, it is to be noted that the Republicans have been consistently more active in business and farm groups. Because many of them are employed in business and farm enterprise, this is not unexpected. Accordingly, the fact that a larger percentage of the 1951 Democrats are members of professional groups can be attributed to the growing predominance of lawyers among them.[8] But we also observe that Democrats as well as Republicans show quite poorly in labor organizations. Since the Democratic party in New York has been traditionally supported by the labor unions, this finding was not anticipated. We can speculate that the middle-class professional strivings of such persons inhibit this kind of an association.

Of further interest in Table 13 are the leadership abilities of legislators. Overall, the Republicans evidence a greater percentage of leadership positions in a greater variety of organizations. This is still the case in 1951 when the Democrats had caught up with and surpassed the Republicans in the number of organizational affiliations. On the basis of this information, it can be suggested that members of the Republican party not only show superior leadership qualities but that their organizational ties go deeper—a further manifestation of their strong "grassroots" perspective. In this light, it would be useful to consider the testimony of a former New York Democratic lawmaker:

[In New York City] most people don't know what an Assemblyman is. He is in no sense a community leader. . . . He is not the kind of community leader in the city which is outside the city. Outside the city, an Assemblyman is a substantial person. He's a prominent person. One of the reasons is that the Assemblymen from the upstate communities are apt to have an interest in representing their districts which

8. See Table 16.

is different from that of other Assemblymen in any other district.[9]

## POLITICAL PARTY LEADERSHIP

Organized groups strive for direct access to government in order that they may better influence public decision-making. For the most part, they focus on those features of governmental policy which bear directly on their special interests. At this point we should recognize that political parties are very similar to interest groups in that they too have certain stakes that they seek to protect or promote through governmental action. Referring to this, V. O. Key states: "The [party] organization may be considered, in effect, as a pressure group that desires to control the selection of as many public employees as possible and to control the distribution of other favors as perquisites in which the members of the party hierarchy have an interest."[10] Among those things which the party attempts to control in the legislature are decisions affecting state judgeships, legislative apportionment, and public works, to name a few. Such matters are the source of many important rewards which party leaders depend upon if they are to hold their organizations together. Hence there is good cause to account for the number of legislators who are also leaders of the extra-legislative party organizations.

Another reason for scrutinizing such ties is that a lawmaker can assert considerably greater independence when he is his own county or district party leader. This is aptly illustrated by the observations of Warren Moscow:

Fred Young, of Lewis County, was one state Senator who was frequently independent of his legislative leadership and of the leadership of the party in the state, but he never

9. Ludwig Teller, "Reminiscences," p. 226.
10. *Politics, Parties and Pressure Groups* (New York: Thomas Y. Crowell, 1958), pp. 381–82.

disagreed with his county chairman. After he received orders
from the majority leader to vote for a measure he did not
like, he would go through the motion of calling his home
town and would emerge from the telephone booth saying
he had been in conference with his county chairman, and
his chairman had told him to vote against the leadership on
the bill. Young, of course, was county chairman of Lewis
County.[11]

The data in Table 14 show a significant overlapping
of legislators and party officers.[12] In addition, party interests are better represented in 1951 than in 1931 as evidenced by an increase of 21 percent to 28 percent. The
greatest gains were made among the most influential party
leaders—county chairmen and district leaders.[13] In partial

Table 14. Percentage of 1931 and 1951 Legislators Who Showed
          Leadership in Party Organizations, Classified by Political
          Party.

| Type of party leadership | 1931 legislators | | | 1951 legislators | | |
|---|---|---|---|---|---|---|
| | Dem. | Repub. | All | Dem. | Repub. | All |
| State committee chmn. | —% | —% | —% | —% | 1% | 1% |
| County chmn. or leaders | — | 11 | 6 | 1 | 14 | 9 |
| District, ward and city leaders | 12 | 1 | 6 | 20 | 3 | 10 |
| State committeemen | 2 | 4 | 3 | — | 4 | 2 |
| Other officers—national, county or local | 2 | 8 | 6 | 8 | 5 | 6 |
| Total | 16% | 24% | 21% | 29% | 27% | 28% |

Note: Legislators are categorized according to the highest party
position achieved in their political careers.

11. Warren Moscow, pp. 174–75.
12. As almost all legislators are members of party committees or clubs
—the lower levels of the party structure—we focus only on party leadership positions, the higher levels of party structure.
13. Since Democrats are based primarily within New York City, an
area of only five counties, it is the district leaders rather than county
leaders who are most prevalent among them. Because the Republicans
are predominantly from the more rural part of the state, where their
constituencies are spread among 57 counties, there is a considerably
greater proportion of them who have been county chairmen.

explanation of this trend, it can be suggested that as the remuneration for legislative office increases, the party chieftains are strongly tempted to reserve such positions for themselves. The story is told that when Governor Dewey considered doubling legislative salaries in the mid-1950s, the lawmakers resisted for reasons other than parsimony.

> Governor Dewey insisted on the increase from $5,000 to $10,000, but upstate legislators pleaded with him to recede, to make it $7,500 because they were afraid that if it were $10,000 their leaders would want the jobs for themselves. So it was reduced to $7,500, I believe virtually at the last minute.[14]

Another consideration in viewing our statistics is to note the inroads that have been made by those who tend to place high regard on the patronage aspects of public institutions. In this way we can begin to account for the absence of a strong ideological orientation among the lawmakers. That is, when acting on various issues, legislators usually generate the greatest interest in the very practical questions of political leverage and reward.

## PARTICIPATION IN BANKING AND CORPORATE ENTERPRISE

At the forefront of the forces engaged in a continuous battle for legislative influence at Albany are found a score or more of lobby groups representing the interests controlling money and industry. In the wealthiest and most highly industrialized state in the Union, it is no accident that those who dominate the fields of investment and production of consumers' goods should thus exercise tremendous pressure.

Such is the appraisal made by Belle Zeller in her study of

---

14. Ludwig Teller, p. 291.

*Pressure Politics in New York.*[15] And such is the rationale with which we examine the financial and corporate connections of the legislators.

The significance of such a survey is dramatically illustrated by an incident which took place in 1934. At that time, it was revealed that the chairman of the New York Senate Committee on Public Service was closely associated with certain utility interests. In a letter to the vice-president of the Associated Gas and Electric Company, Senator Warren T. Thayer revealed the degree to which he was accessible to this utility: "The Legislature adjourned last Friday. . . . I hope my work during the past session was satisfactory to your company, not so much for the new legislation enacted, but from the fact that many detrimental bills were introduced we were able to kill in my committee."[16] After this revelation, several lawmakers asked to be excused from voting on utility bills because they were officers, directors, legal advisers or stockholders of utility companies.[17]

In our attempt to measure the extent of such interest affiliations, two basic categories are presented in Table 15. One pertains to the banking industry and the other includes such forms of corporate enterprise as manufacturing establishments, insurance companies, large real-estate companies and public utilities. Upon perusing the data, a major difference between the two parties becomes more clearly evident. Republicans show a high degree of participation in business and financial organizations while the Democratic showing is negligible. This finding was anticipated as we formerly noted that Republican lawmakers tend to be of much higher standing on the occupational class ladder.

---

15. P. 41.
16. The letter was dated March 15, 1927. See State of New York, *Proceeding of the Judiciary Committee of the Senate in the Matter of Investigation Requested by Senator Thayer,* Legislative Document, 1934, No. 102, p. 464.
17. *The New York Times,* April 6, 1934.

Table 15. Number and Percentage of 1931 and 1951 Legislators Who Have Served as Either an Officer, Director or Trustee in Business Enterprise.

| Type of business unit | 1931 legislators | | | 1951 legislators | | |
|---|---|---|---|---|---|---|
| | Dem. | Repub. | All | Dem. | Repub. | All |
| Banking | | | | | | |
| percentage | 4% | 27% | 16% | 4% | 23% | 15% |
| number | 4 | 29 | 33 | 3 | 28 | 31 |
| Corporations | | | | | | |
| percentage | 4% | 18% | 11% | 1% | 6% | 4% |
| number | 4 | 19 | 23 | 1 | 7 | 8 |

Note: The business affiliations of lawmakers are scrutinized during their entire political career. A legislator could be assigned to more than one category.

But, in addition, our data can be seen as further manifestation of the long-time collusion between Republicanism and business in the State of New York. In the early part of the twentieth century, upstate candidates for office who were unwilling to recognize such ties could find it tough going.

> . . . in those early days, back in 1908, 1909, 1910 . . . powerful people in the corporations, mostly politically related to Thomas C. Platt, the [Republican] boss, had begun to control legislation, particularly the legislation favorable to the corporations.[18]

> The forces that were opposed to me and to my nomination [to the legislature] were the corporations. At that time the gas and electric corporation of Utica more or less controlled the conventions and the elections. They were against me. I think the first general public speech I made was on the growing power of corporations in politics in this country. . . .[19]

18. Frederick M. Davenport, "Reminiscences." Columbia University Oral History Collection, Special Collections, Butler Library, p. 44.
    19. Ibid., p. 38.

So it was the case in those years that large business units had a hand in establishing criteria for Republican candidate eligibility. This was evidently the situation, still, in the 1920s and 1930s: political aspirants selected often had very substantial and direct connections with the business community. But while corporate attachments have diminished considerably of late, the banking ties of Republicans seem to persist.

In light of this, it comes as no surprise that, in the fall of 1963, the press disclosed that seven state lawmakers (four of them Republicans) and their wives had attended a combination banking convention and Caribbean cruise. Among the guests were three members of the legislature's banking committees. Most revealing is the fact that the whole six-day luxury affair to Nassau and back was paid for by the Savings Banks Association of New York State and its member banks. The reaction of one State Senator who attended was: "Why bring it up now? These trips have been going on for seventeen years."[20]

## OCCUPATIONAL INTERESTS

In American society, there is the long-standing conception that the legislator has a different status than either the administrator in the executive branch or the judge. Only the lawmaker has been given the right to continue in his occupation while holding public office. The expectation is that, when elected, he would continue as butcher, baker, farmer, or lawyer and so better represent his constituency and its economy. Thus, lawmaking in New York,

20. Paul Tillet (ed.), *The Political Vocation* (New York: Basic Books, 1965), p. 457. Also reported in *The New York Times,* October 25, 1963. It might be interesting to note the scolding *Times* editorial of that date: "Inasmuch as new banking legislation comes before every Assembly session, it seems a safe, nay, an inescapable, assumption that this was a case of the legislators going to a lobby instead of a lobby going to a Legislature. Of course some legislators are—as bank directors or counsel for banks—practically members of the lobby anyway."

as in all states, is essentially a part-time responsibility. The legislature is generally in session three months a year when both houses usually meet only two or three days a week.

Table 16 gives us some indication of occupational representation in the legislative chambers. It is apparent that lawyers have maintained a strong hold and, over a twenty-year period, were able to increase their proportion of seats

Table 16. Occupations of 1931 and 1951 Legislators, Classified by Political Party.

| Occupations | 1931 legislators | | | 1951 legislators | | |
|---|---|---|---|---|---|---|
| | Dem. | Repub. | All | Dem. | Repub. | All |
| Farmers | 1% | 20% | 11% | —% | 8% | 4% |
| Lawyers | 59 | 35 | 46 | 76 | 40 | 55 |
| Newspaper men | 1 | 1 | 1 | — | 2 | 2 |
| Other professional men | 7 | 3 | 5 | 3 | 5 | 4 |
| Bankers | 1 | 7 | 4 | — | 5 | 3 |
| Contractors | 1 | 2 | 2 | — | 1 | 1 |
| Manufacturing & industry | 4 | 7 | 6 | 2 | 3 | 2 |
| Insurance and/or real estate | 12 | 4 | 7 | 4 | 10 | 7 |
| Merchants | 3 | 14 | 9 | 5 | 17 | 12 |
| Salesmen and clerks | 6 | 1 | 4 | 5 | 2 | 3 |
| Skilled and unskilled workers | 2 | 2 | 2 | 1 | 2 | 1 |
| Minor professional & technical | 2 | 4 | 3 | 3 | 5 | 4 |
| Others* | — | 1 | 1 | 1 | 1 | 1 |
| Total percent | 99% | 101% | 101% | 100% | 101% | 99% |

*This includes housewives.

from 46 percent to 55 percent. Merchants, real estate, and insurance men have also been strong in numbers, though they lag far behind members of the bar. The once prominent farmers appear to be in a state of decline.

Not to be overlooked in the findings is the fact that just about every one of our subjects was privately employed while at the same time serving in a public role. Such sweeping prevalence of sideline legislators well illustrates the problem of conflicts-of-interest. For the question arises whether the public servant should disassociate himself from a bill because it affects his occupational interest or whether, as an experienced person in the field, he can make a greater contribution by participating. Should a real estate broker who has greater knowledge of mortgages than others be permitted to sit on the Mortgage and Real Estate Committee? If this seems warranted, what should that person do when a bill comes along which would benefit him directly? This matter becomes even more intricate when we note that lawyers earn much of their livelihood representing private clients in cases dealing with the same state statutes they helped to pass.

## ETHICS AND LEGISLATORS

At this point in our analysis, it would be useful to make some general assessment of the extent to which there is indeed a problem of ethics among New York lawmakers. It was the legislature itself that said in the preamble to the 1954 Code of Ethics that "the people are entitled to expect from their public servants a set of standards above the morals of the market place." Yet in tracing the political careers of legislators, we find that a surprisingly high percentage of them fall far short of such a goal.

Table 17 reveals that among the 1931 personnel, approximately 13 percent of the Democrats had been judged guilty of some kind of disreputable activity while serving either as lawmakers or subsequently in other public office. Only three percent of the Republicans were so implicated. In most instances, the resultant penalty was disbarment from the legal profession where the defendants had been accused of such things as "ambulance-chasing," mishandling of fees, and perjury. In addition, about three percent of the Democrats and two percent of the Republicans were convicted of such crimes as income-tax evasion, disorderly conduct, and violation of the Hatch Act;[21] and one percent of the membership of both parties were dismissed because of misconduct in the administration of public duties. We also count the case of a Democrat who had committed suicide upon the presentation of a grand jury indictment. Though he was yet to have his full day in court, we include him here because of the extreme manner in which he reacted to the indictment—an indication there was some substance to the charges. It is inter-

Table 17. Social Mobility and Unethical Behavior Among 1931 and 1951 Legislators, Classified by Political Party

| | 1931 legislators | | | | 1951 legislators | | | |
| | Dem. | | Repub. | | Dem. | | Repub. | |
| | N | % | N | % | N | % | N | % |
|---|---|---|---|---|---|---|---|---|
| Unethical conduct | | | | | | | | |
| Disbarment | 7 | 7.4 | — | — | 1 | 1.2 | — | — |
| Criminal conviction | 3 | 3.2 | 2 | 1.9 | 2 | 2.4 | 3 | 2.5 |
| Misconduct in office | 1 | 1.1 | 1 | .9 | 1 | 1.2 | 2 | 1.7 |
| Suicide under indictment | 1 | 1.1 | — | — | 1 | 1.2 | — | — |
| Total | 12 | 12.8% | 3 | 2.8 | 5 | 6.0% | 5 | 4.2 |
| Level of social mobility* | | | | | | | | |
| High | 4 | | — | | 1 | | 1 | |
| Medium high | 5 | | — | | 4 | | 3 | |
| Medium low | 1 | | — | | — | | 1 | |
| Low | — | | 3 | | — | | — | |
| Unknown | 2 | | — | | — | | — | |
| Total | 12 | | 3 | | 5 | | 5 | |

Note: These figures are complete as of 1968.

* High mobiles are those of low social origins. Low mobiles are those of high social origins. Medium high and medium low are intermediate points between the two extremes. The criteria for assessing level of social mobility are occupation of father or initial occupation of the legislator and ethnic origins, e.g., foreign-born stock, old American stock.

21. The Hatch Political Activities Act forbids federal employees to take any active part "in political management or in political campaigns."

esting to note, furthermore, that though a great deal of corrupt activity was uncovered among the New York City Democrats by a state investigating committee in the early 1930s (known as the Seabury investigations) , none of the 1931 Democratic legislators were convicted at that time. Instead, evidence of unethical behavior in one form or another has emerged slowly through time.

How can we account for the very poor showing of the Democratic party during the 1930s and 1940s? At least part of the answer can be discerned by an examination of the social bases of the two partisan organizations. In an earlier chapter, it was noted that the Republicans have been recruited largely from among old-stock Americans of middle to high social standing, i.e., middle to low mobiles.[22] The Democrats, on the other hand, have attracted mostly urban persons of low social beginnings, i.e., high mobiles. In his study of urban slums, the sociologist William F. Whyte explains the significance of this:

> The Irish and later immigrant peoples have had the greatest difficulty in finding places for themselves in our urban social and economic structure. Does anyone believe that the immigrants and their children could have achieved their present degree of social mobility without gaining control of the political organization of some of our largest cities? The same is true of the racket organization. Politics and the rackets have furnished an important means of social mobility for individuals, who, because of their ethnic backgrounds and low class position, are blocked from advancement in the "respectable channels."[23]

---

22. The indices for assessing level of social mobility in this study are occupation of father or initial occupation of the legislator and ethnic origins. By the term "low mobiles," we refer to those of high social beginnings. "High mobiles" are those of low social origins; and "medium mobiles" would be located at the intermediate point between both extremes.

23. "Social Organization in the Slums," *The American Sociological Review* 8 (February, 1943) : 38.

Given the social background and status strivings of most New York Democrats, we can better understand their behavior. Some, in their desire to climb the heights, show little regard for the requisites of civic virtue; or, at the opportune moment, they revert to the norms of the racket organization. In a book entitled *Power, Corruption, and Rectitude,* Arnold Rogow and Harold Lasswell refer to such persons as "gain" and "game" politicians.[24] It is their contention that early deprivation of the personality system may eventually lead to corruption. Thus "game" activists are described as persons who are essentially concerned with manipulating voters and cliques as a way of attaining the respect and affection they sorely need; "gain" activists are persons who are preoccupied with graft and riches as the means of feeding their need for security and well-being. Our own data seem to confirm the greater vulnerability of the latter type which we label "high" and "medium-high" mobiles, i.e., individuals of low social origins who are apt to have experienced deprivation of "welfare values." Relevant to this is the economic bleakness of depression days during the 1930s, a condition likely to accentuate feelings of loss and insecurity.

In viewing the record for the 1951 lawmakers, it can be argued that though percentages of six for the Democrats and four for the Republicans still reflect a grim situation, a general improvement in the moral climate of the legislature is evident. (At least as it is measured by our rather crude indices.) In pondering this change, we must bear in mind that legislator-politicians no longer begin as low on the socio-economic ladder as formerly; and the prosperity of the post-World War II years has undoubtedly helped to placate the ambitions of such persons much more effectively than could have possibly been the case during the 1930s.

---

24. *Power, Corruption, and Rectitude* (Englewood Cliffs, N.J.: Prentice-Hall, Inc. 1963), pp. 44–55.

With reference to party performance, we should recognize that as the social gap between Republicans and Democrats has narrowed, differences in the moral standards of the two partisan groups are no longer as great. But it must also be understood that politicians of higher status and education can be more sophisticated in the pursuit of their own interests. "Honest graft"[25] and the "legal bribe"[26] are still very much in practice, but very difficult to detect and account for in any definitive way. As illustrated in the conclusions which follow, a serious problem in the State of New York has been to limit such practices effectively.

## CONCLUSION: A CODE OF ETHICS?

We have seen that the organizational life of New York legislators is a rich and varied one. And while this may enhance the representative function of such persons, it presents problems as well—i.e., problems of conflicts-of-interest. Because the organizational experience of Democrats tends to differ from that of Republicans, furthermore, the subject of conflicts-of-interest applies somewhat differently to each of the party memberships. The former are oriented more toward ethnic and religious associations, a reflection of the party's constituency base. The latter appear to be more concerned with business, farm, and fraternal groups. Pertinent is the fact that Republicans seem to be deeply involved with banks and, to a lesser extent, with business corporations, i.e., manufacturing, insurance, utility, and large real estate companies. Many

---

25. This is a phrase coined by the late Senator Plunkitt of Tammany Hall in which he describes how the purchase of real estate for public improvement provided opportunity for party members to enrich themselves. Other types of contractual arrangements with government can also be included when using the term. Plunkitt is quoted in W. L. Riordan, *Plunkitt of Tammany Hall* (New York: Alfred A. Knopf, 1948), pp. 3–7.

26. This has reference to the offering of legal fees, retainers, and employment to legislators as a means of influencing legislation.

of them have served as officers, directors, or trustees of such institutions. As a related dimension, it should also be recalled that almost all the lawmakers hold other occupations while serving a public role; and while the profession of law predominates in both parties, it was earlier discerned that the Republicans are, for the most part, of higher status in the practice of this profession than are the Democrats. In addition, many more Republicans are businessmen and farmers (a rapidly diminishing group) as compared to the opposition.

Partly as a consequence of such patterns, Democrats have been more apt to find themselves in serious trouble than has been the case for Republicans. Striving for upward social mobility, usually through the combination of law and politics, Democrats have been more vulnerable to the temptations of material rewards—i.e., many have been caught breaking the law or some other fundamental code. A greater proportion of Republicans, on the other hand, are persons who have "arrived." As indicated by their affiliations, a large number of them have personal stakes in the banks and large businesses. Thus the temptations which Republicans face have been less implicating—i.e., business favoritism in the course of legislation does not lead to convictions.

It is difficult to say whether such party patterns will persist into the future, especially when it is considered that associational and status differences between the two memberships are diminishing. But the occupational and interest attachments of all lawmakers continue unremittingly and, consequently, a troubling question that remains to be answered is what to do about it, if anything. This was the question posed for Governor Thomas E. Dewey when, during the last years of his administration (he served from 1942 to 1954) it was discovered that some of New York's most important politicians, including members of the legislature, owned stock in the state-regulated harness tracks. A public investigation into the matter soon produced new and unexpected testimony that the leader of the Senate had consulted with a convicted racketeer at Sing Sing about a labor problem in his district. To assuage the public in the wake of these scandals, the legislature created a twelve-member study commission "to define by appropriate legislation those businesses and professional activities which are improper for government and party officers." The Lockwood Committee, named after the chairman Charles Lockwood, consisted of eight legislators, thus assuring legislative influence on the standards of conduct to be recommended. Accordingly, in 1954, there was adopted a code of ethics and special committees on ethics were established in the Assembly and the Senate respectively. The code provided for conflicts-of-interest in the following way:

> No . . . member of the legislature or legislative employee should have any interest, financial or otherwise, direct or indirect, or engage in any business or transaction or professional activity or incur any obligation of any nature, which is in substantial conflict with the proper discharge of his duties in the public interest.[27]

In addition, state employees with more than $10,000 interest in any activity regulated by the state were required to report that holding to the Secretary of State; and legislators were prohibited from appearing as lawyers before state agencies on a contingent fee basis. (Contingent, in other words, on how successful they are in representing their private clients.)

But in spite of these provisions, a near steady flow of allegations continued to be highlighted in the newspapers. Most prominent, during the 1962 legislative session, were hearings in the Assembly's ethics committee on charges

---

27. State of New York, *Public Officers Law*, Sec. 74—Code of Ethics.

that the Speaker of the Assembly, Joseph Carlino (a member of our 1951 sample), had violated his oath of office in pushing through legislation for a state fallout shelter program while he was director of a fallout shelter construction company. The Speaker denied any impropriety and was exonerated. In 1963, it was the Senate's turn. The Majority Leader of that chamber, Walter Mahoney (a member of our 1951 sample), came under attack for representing a finance company that benefited from state legislation. He too was exonerated after an inquiry was made by the Manhattan District Attorney.

The embarrassment of such events, however, gave the legislature little choice but to reconsider its code of ethics. With respect to this, the Speaker candidly admitted that outside help would be needed since "any determinations by legislators in the present atmosphere would be viewed with scorn and disbelief."[28] Thus, a special three-man committee of outsiders was selected to hold hearings and make recommendations. Headed by Cloyd Laporte, the chairman of the New York Board of Ethics and a law partner of former Governor Dewey, the ethics committee subsequently presented the following proposals.[29]

1. Members of the legislature and legislative employees should be prohibited from practicing before most state agencies for a fee.

2. Members of the legislature and legislative employees should be prohibited from appearing before the Court of Claims—the state tribunal which hears all claims against the state and awards public funds.

3. Members of the legislature and legislative employees should be prohibited from soliciting or accepting gifts of

28. *Newsweek*, November 11, 1963, p. 33.
29. New York State, *Report of the Special Committee on Ethics*, Legislative Document No. 42, March 1964, pp. 3-7. The other two members of the committee were State Comptroller Arthur Levitt and Cornell University law professor Gray Thoron.

substantial value in which it could be reasonably inferred that the gifts were intended to influence the performance of official duties.

4. Members of the legislature should disclose any interests which may conflict with pending legislation and failure to do so would be a violation of the law punishable as a misdemeanor. Further, the $10,000 minimum interest requiring disclosure be eliminated and that a requirement of annual filing be established.

5. An advisory six-member State Ethics Commission be established to provide machinery for continuing guidance on ethical standards.

This, then, is the "model" code which has attracted the support of a number of good government groups. The legislature itself, reacting to the urgings and goadings of the press and civic organizations, has reluctantly adopted some, but not all, of the recommendations. That which remains taboo is the proposal which would prohibit appearances by legislators before state agencies for a fee— apparently because too many legislators' law practices are dependent on such business.[30] There is also considerable resistance to the creation of a state commission which would police ethical standards. As one close observer notes, "An ethics commission drawing its power and members from outside the Legislature would threaten the system. It is this threat to their positions that prompts legislators to vehement opposition to an ethics commission."[31]

An alternative to this type of ethics control, other than to ignore the subject entirely, is to make legislative service a full-time occupation with appropriate salaries. (What is "appropriate" would, of course, be another problem.) The

---

30. Joseph Carlino, the former Assembly Speaker, testifies to this. See Howard G. Paster, "Ethics in Albany" (unpublished master's thesis, Columbia University, 1967) , p. 22.

31. Howard G. Paster's observation, *ibid.*, p. 23.

rationale to this is that by limiting active private interests, the conflicts would be minimized. To quote George Metcalf, a former State Senator: "The first thing is to give up the notion he (a legislator) can wear two hats—one public and one private. He needs two toppers about as much as he needs two heads."[32]

32. The New York *Herald Tribune*, January 21, 1964.

# 5

# ADIEU TO LEGISLATIVE OFFICE

Taking leave of the New York Legislature is always a sentimental occurrence, for in this place, the longer the tenure, the stronger the attachments of loyalty and camaraderie that usually develop. But of course, irrespective of such feelings, all lawmakers must eventually depart and when this happens some revealing questions can then be asked. Perhaps most important is to inquire *how* they leave and *why*.

## HOW LEGISLATORS LEAVE

In a study of eight state legislatures which was conducted in the late 1930s, it was found that "an enormous proportion of those who leave the legislature do so without a battle for renomination or reelection."[1] Perplexed, the author states: "The real task . . . is to find why so many legislators . . . choose not to run again."[2]

Our own data, as seen in Table 18, fully confirms the findings of this earlier investigation. Among New York lawmakers, fewer than 20 percent have left the legislature because of defeat at the polls—an indication of the very passive role which the electorate actually performs in the

---

1. Charles S. Hyneman, p. 27.
2. *Ibid.*, p. 30.

legislative process.[3] As a source of democratic control, party primary elections appear to be even less effective. Primaries, i.e., intraparty elections for the nomination of candidates, were instituted at the turn of the century to undermine boss rule and to assure greater participation by the rank and file in party affairs. Yet, only nine percent of the 1931 personnel lost their seats this way and in 1951 the percentage is a paltry five. Overall, using the criteria of primary and election defeats, politics in the legislature and in the state seems to have become even less competitive over time.

Table 18. Means by Which Legislators Leave the Legislature: A Comparison of 1931 and 1951 Personnel.

| Means of leaving | 1931 legislators | | | 1951 legislators | | |
|---|---|---|---|---|---|---|
| | Dem. | Repub. | All | Dem. | Repub. | All |
| Election defeat | 21% | 18% | 19% | 17% | 15% | 16% |
| Primary defeat | 8 | 10 | 9 | 6 | 5 | 5 |
| Death | 11 | 9 | 10 | 13 | 13 | 13 |
| Resignation | 60 | 63 | 62 | 50 | 63 | 58 |
| Still in legislature | — | — | — | 14 | 4 | 8 |
| Total percent | 100% | 100% | 100% | 100% | 100% | 100% |

Note: Legislators are accounted for up to 1967.

Of the remaining legislators, a little more than ten percent died while occupying a place in the lawmaking body. But of major significance is the fact that a majority of them, around 60 percent for both sample sessions, simply resigned from office. For one reason or another, most of them expressed the desire to leave and did so. How can this be explained?

3. Of course, the voting control of the citizenry may have its indirect effects. It can be argued that a lawmaker may not wander too far from the expectations and desires of his constituents without fear of defeat at the next election.

## WHY LEGISLATORS RESIGN

### Political advancement

It is evident in Table 19 that the preponderant number of all retired representatives advance, or attempt to advance, into other public office. For the most part, such movement is direct—the persons involved drop their legislative roles and, at the appropriate time, step unerringly into other public offices. For a much smaller number, there is an element of uncertainty; here they resign and then spend a period of time either waiting or maneuvering before they resume their political pursuits.

Table 19. Percentage of Resigned Legislators Who Advanced or Attempted to Advance, Directly and Indirectly, into Office.

| Advancement Pattern | 1931 legislators | | | 1951 legislators | | |
|---|---|---|---|---|---|---|
| | Dem. | Repub. | All | Dem. | Repub. | All |
| Direct advancement or attempted advancement | 59% | 36% | 47% | 81% | 34% | 51% |
| Indirect advancement or attempted advancement | 11% | 15% | 13% | 2% | 5% | 4% |
| Total percent | 70% | 51% | 60% | 83% | 39% | 55% |
| Total number | 39 | 34 | 73 | 36 | 30 | 66 |

Note: Legislators accounted for up to 1967.

We see, then, that one important reason why incumbents do not return to the legislative chambers is that they have other places to go. For many of them, legislative office is but a way-station where they can establish eligibility for more desirable positions on the political career ladder. The act of departure, in such cases, is probably planned and anticipated from the moment of first arrival in the legislature. In speaking of "more desirable positions," reference is to other offices which are generally perceived as being more rewarding with respect to either prestige, money or political security; the most sought-after positions usually manifest a combination of all these qualities.

It should be noted, furthermore, that advancement is much more prominent among the Democrats than among the Republicans. Why it is that the former manifest this keen desire to go elsewhere will be examined later in the study.

## The age cycle

A man's political career is also contingent on his age. There are numerous occasions when a politician declares that he no longer has the time or energy to devote to public duty. This can often be interpreted as a tactic of political interplay whereby the representative tests his popularity among his constituents. At other times, however, he speaks his true feelings and is, in effect, signifying that he has become too old to play the game.

A perplexing problem is to discern that old age is the real reason for resigning. In American society, sixty-five years is the generally accepted age for the relinquishment of life's major responsibilities. If we accept this standard, it would then be reasonable to assume that any legislator who abandons public life when he is around sixty-five years does so because he is past his prime and is unwilling to continue.

Table 20 provides some insight into the relationship of age and retirement. Here we are concerned only with those legislators who vacated their seats and never again achieved, or tried to achieve, governmental office. It is apparent from the data that the age factor has greater relevance to the Republicans than to the Democrats. As previously discerned, the average Republican arrives and sits in the legislature towards the twilight of his life-cycle; consequently, he is confronted with a more limited range of subsequent political opportunities. As a member of what has been the majority party, moreover, he had good reason to remain in the lawmaking body right to the very end. On the other end of the scale, it is seen that roughly half of the Democrats retire when under forty-five years. Apparently, when the average Democrat retires from politics, it is usually for reasons other than the fact that he is too old to participate.

Table 20. Resignation of 1931 and 1951 Legislators Who Evidence No Extra-Legislative Political Mobility.

| Age of legislative resignation | 1931 legislators | | | 1951 legislators | | |
|---|---|---|---|---|---|---|
| | Dem. | Repub. | All | Dem. | Repub. | All |
| Minus 34 yrs. | 5% | —% | 2% | 29% | —% | 4% |
| 35 to 44 yrs. | 50 | 9 | 24 | 14 | 4 | 6 |
| 45 to 54 yrs. | 15 | 24 | 21 | 43 | 11 | 15 |
| 55 to 64 yrs. | 5 | 27 | 19 | — | 24 | 21 |
| 65 yrs. plus | 25 | 33 | 30 | 14 | 57 | 51 |
| Unknown | — | 6 | 4 | — | 4 | 4 |
| Total percent | 100% | 99% | 100% | 100% | 100% | 101% |
| Total number | 20 | 33 | 53 | 7 | 46 | 53 |

Of additional interest is that when we compare the 1931 figures with those for 1951, the two parties appear to be following opposite courses. Age as a cause of retirement has played an increasingly prominent role among the Republicans while the reverse is true of the Democrats.

## DEFEAT AT THE POLLS

Early in the chapter, we took note of the fact that relatively few personnel leave the legislature because of election defeat. It would be useful at this time to take a closer look at those who do leave this way. What are the conditions which underlie such dire happenings?

## The impact of national politics

In his very fine book on state politics, V. O. Key asks to what extent there is "An Autonomous State Politics."[4] He contends that many states outside of the one-party South and New England "tend to be carried along by the great swings of political cycles which mark the alteration in dominance of Democrats and Republicans on the national scene. The capacity of the state to act independently of national issues and with a focus on state questions withers as the affairs of states are swept by the tides of national politics."[5]

In support of Professor Key's thesis, Table 21 shows that state legislative candidates who are associated with the defeated party on the national level must often bear the consequences of such an affiliation. In viewing the 1931 Republicans, it is seen that 19 out of 20 who lost at the polls were deposed between 1931 and 1934—five of them were defeated in the presidential election year of 1932. Plagued by economic depression, the early 1930s represented a time when the tide had run out for the Republicans all across the nation. Accordingly, it was during this very same period that in New York the Democrats took control of the Assembly (in 1935) and the Senate (1933 to 1938) for the first time since 1913, the year Woodrow Wilson began his first term as a Democratic President of the United States.

The effects of the "tides of national politics" can be more readily discerned in the electoral statistics for the 1951 legislators. Here we see that the Democrats suffered their greatest losses in 1952 and 1956, the very years when Eisenhower led the Republican national ticket. More recently, in 1964, the Republicans were subjected to the severe effects of Goldwater's presidential candidacy.

All this aptly demonstrates an important aspect of the

4. V. O. Key, Chapter 2.
5. Ibid., p. 28.

Table 21. Percentage Distribution of Election Defeats of 1931 and 1951 Legislators over Time.

| Year of election defeat | Democrats | | Republicans | |
|---|---|---|---|---|
| | N | % | N | % |
| **1931 legislators** | | | | |
| 1931 | 2 | 10 | 3 | 15 |
| 1932 | 4 | 20 | 5 | 25 |
| 1933 | 8 | 40 | 5 | 25 |
| 1934 | — | — | 6 | 30 |
| 1935 | 1 | 5 | — | — |
| 1936 | — | — | 1 | 5 |
| Later years | 5 | 25 | — | — |
| Total | 20 | 100% | 20 | 100% |
| **1951 legislators** | | | | |
| 1952 | 12 | 75 | 1 | 6 |
| 1954 | — | — | 2 | 11 |
| 1956 | 3 | 19 | — | — |
| 1958 | — | — | 2 | 11 |
| 1960 | — | — | 2 | 11 |
| 1962 | 1 | 6 | — | — |
| 1964 | — | — | 10 | 55 |
| 1966 | — | — | 1 | 6 |
| Total | 16 | 100% | 18 | 100% |

Note: Under the provisions of the New York Constitution, members of the Assembly were elected for one year terms until 1938 when a constitutional amendment increased the terms to two years. Members of the Senate have been elected for two-year terms since 1846.

democratic process. There is the common assumption, for the most part an untested one, that each candidate for public office is judged according to his qualifications and performance. In New York, it is more often the case that the electorate is influenced by matters of national scope which are external to the functioning of the legislature. Sometimes, even the candidates have difficulty understanding or accepting this. For example, Edward Costikyan, a former leader of the Manhattan Democrats, relates the story of a young man making his first run for the Assembly. Having prepared himself with speeches, the candidate soon noticed that the party organization neither called upon him at rallies nor referred to him in the campaign literature. Worried, he began badgering his district leader and soon drew a response. The leader asked if he had ever seen the East River ferryboat docks.

"Yes," he answered.

And when the ferryboats come in, do "you see the water suck in behind?"

"Yes."

"And when the water sucks in behind the ferryboat, all kinds of dirty garbage comes smack into the slip with the ferryboat?"

"Yes."

"So go home and relax. Al Smith (the presidential candidate) is the ferryboat. This year you're the garbage."[6]

## The impact of reform politics

Close examination of Table 21 reveals that while the Republicans took some heavy losses in the early 1930s, so too did the Democrats. Most striking is the fact that eight out of twenty election defeats occurred in the year 1933. What was responsible for this? Why didn't the 1932 Democratic national victory have any effect?

Answers to these questions can be found in the history of New York. Of significance was a series of investigations of New York City government which were conducted by a joint committee of the state legislature. Known as the Seabury investigations, they revealed extensive corruption of the city's officialdom including those at the very top of the governmental structure.[7] Implicated also was the Democratic party, the organization which had recruited

6. See *Behind Closed Doors*, pp. 325–26.
7. See New York State, Joint Legislative Committee to Investigate the Affairs of the City of New York: *Report to the Legislature*, December 28, 1932.

and supported these officials. It was not long before a spirit of reform set in; and in 1933, Fiorello H. La Guardia, candidate of the Republican and Fusion parties, was elected Mayor of New York. As the Democratic party was voted out of the city's administration, so too was a sizable portion of the Democratic legislative incumbents. Interestingly enough, only one lawmaker who served in 1931 was subject to serious charges during the Seabury hearings, though he was never convicted.

This illustrates a significant phenomenon of the American scene. Ultimately, it is the electorate that controls and when it becomes clearly evident that the party organization has gone beyond acceptable limits, the electorate can be aroused. It is then that the movement for reform takes its toll. The strongly felt indignation of the public and the sudden need to moralize politics typically takes on anti-organization qualities. At such times, all members of the implicated party are affected and many of them, whether personally guilty or not, go down to defeat.

## Finality of electoral defeat

Finally, as a way of assessing the long-run impact of the ballot, we inquire: of all those lawmakers who were turned down by the voters, how many managed to return to government service? Table 22 indicates that more than half were able to return at a later date. In addition, most of such legislators were subsequently appointed to office rather than elected. Thus, largely through the powers of appointment—or as some would say, the distribution of patronage—a decision made by the electorate can be modified.

It is evident, then, that failure at the polls does not necessarily signify the end of a politician's career. Many of them have the peculiar knack of perpetuating themselves in the political system with or without the consent of the governed. It is largely this characteristic which

Table 22. Number and Percent of Defeated Legislators Returned
to Office.

| | Democrats | | Republicans | | All | |
|---|---|---|---|---|---|---|
| | N | % | N | % | N | % |
| 1931 returnees | | | | | | |
| Appointed | 8 | 40 | 8 | 40 | 16 | 40 |
| Elected | 2 | 10 | 3 | 15 | 5 | 13 |
| Total | 10 | 50% | 11 | 55% | 21 | 53% |
| 1951 returnees | | | | | | |
| Appointed | 6 | 35 | 7 | 39 | 13 | 37 |
| Elected | 4 | 24 | 1 | 5 | 5 | 14 |
| Total | 10 | 59% | 8 | 44% | 18 | 51% |

Note: Legislators accounted for up to 1967.

highlights the fact that the average New York legislator
is very much the professional politician—with great persistence, he fights to stay alive in the give-and-take of politics. We'll have more to say about this in the next chapter.

## CONCLUSION: THE CONSENT OF THE GOVERNED

One of the basic tenets of democratic theory is the
doctrine of the consent of the governed. As it was expressed
in the Declaration of Independence, the idea of consent
calls for the accountability of governors to the citizenry
and it implies that this accountability is to be secured
through direct popular vote.

Though the electorate may have the power of consent,
its willingness or ability to use it effectivey is another
matter. Indeed, much of the history of New York, as of
most other places, is the attempt to assure greater governmental responsiveness through various adjustments and
reforms. There are no panaceas in such matters and the

tinkering continues even to the present day. With reference to the legislative body, there has probably been as much confusion as there has been enlightenment.

On the assumption that possession of property or payment of taxes makes for reliable citizens, the first state constitution of 1777 provided that members of the Senate as well as the Governor were to be freeholders and were to be elected by freeholders whose property would be valued at 100 pounds over and above all indebtedness. The right to vote for members of the less aristocratic Assembly was limited to persons possessing a twenty-pound freehold or to those having rented a tenement of the value of forty shillings. In addition, Senators were to hold office for four-year terms, twenty-four being apportioned among four large districts. After the first election they were to be divided by lot into four classes, so that the terms of six would expire each year. Assemblymen were to serve for one-year terms, being apportioned to each county according to the number of electors.

By the early nineteenth century, new ideas stressing the "common man" and human equality began to take hold. Reflecting the spirit of "Jacksonian democracy," the Constitutional Convention of 1821 extended the suffrage to include all white men, twenty-one years of age or older, who paid taxes. In addition, the number of senatorial districts was increased to eight with the provision that four Senators would represent a district—one Senator would be elected annually from each district.

The movement to revitalize democratic institutions took an interesting turn with regard to the legislature during the convention of 1846. Consider the following argument as revealed in the records of the debates.

It was important that there should not be so long an interval as four years from the election of a senator until the expiration of his office. A senator might entertain opinions contrary to the well known wishes of his constituents and frequently did mis-represent them. He might have selfish designs, contrary to the public interest, and it was possible he might be corrupt; and if the period of four years were to stand as the term of his office, the people would cease to trouble themselves about him; or they would indulge in useless regrets that they had no means of reaching him till the term of his office expired. By lessening the term one-half, and adopting the single district system, they brought the senator more immediately within the knowledge and observation of his constituents and more immediately responsible to them.[8]

This manner of reasoning prevailed and was subsequently incorporated, not only into the fundamental law of the state, but also into the hearts and minds of men. Short terms of office and the single-district system as a means of keeping elected representatives close to the people became part of the popular perspective and, with few exceptions, these ideas have persisted. With remarkable consistency, proposals to extend the terms of lawmakers have been rejected by the voters, the latest being in 1965. Only in 1937 did it happen that a constitutional amendment was adopted which lengthened the terms of Assemblymen from one to two years, the same as it was in the Senate.

In assessing the time-honored concepts of representative government, the question arises as to how much is truly effective and how much is myth, rooted in the untested value judgments of the people—e.g., there comes to mind the old axiom: "Where annual elections end, tyranny begins." It can be argued that procedures traditionally relied upon have not necessarily provided responsible citizen control over New York's representatives; nor are the latter very intimate with or even known by the electorate. A

8. The report of Mr. W. Taylor from the Committee on Apportionment, Elections and Tenure of the Legislature, *Report of the Debates and Proceedings of the Convention for the Revision of the Constitution of the State of New York, 1846* (Albany: The Evening Atlas, 1846) , p. 373.

survey made by Elmo Roper and Associates found that
only eight percent of New York City voters could identify
the Assemblyman that they voted for in a recent election;
and not more than twenty percent in selected upstate
communities could so identify the candidates.[9] Our own
data has shown that a relatively small proportion of all
New York lawmakers relinquish legislative office because
of election and primary defeats; and among those who are
defeated, many manage to continue their political careers
at some later date with or without voter approval. In
addition, we have seen that success or failure at the polls
is more closely related to the fluctuations of national elections than it is to the personal qualities of the representatives.

Nor can we ignore the high proportion of lawmakers
who have been convicted of ethical lapses (see Table 17).
The fact of the matter is that legislators have not been
subject to the close observation of constituents, but have
enjoyed wide latitude of action in the pursuit of their
private interests. Clearly the time has arrived for a recon-
sideration of the generally accepted techniques of representation. While we have recognized some of the defects
here, remedial proposals will be suggested in the final
chapter of this book.

---

9. Reported in *State Legislatures Progress Reporter* (New York: National Municipal League, January, 1967), pp. 1, 3.

# 6

# POST-LEGISLATIVE PATHWAYS

The motives of persons who enter politics are many and varied. A drive for power or status, a zeal for contention, a concern for ideology, a desire for public service, are among the more commonly cited ones. Those who seek to assuage such feelings through political involvement probably prefer this channel to any other. We should not take too seriously the occasional statements of politicians that they really want to go back to full-time law practice or the insurance business. If this were so, they probably would never have ventured into the public arena in the first place.

Persons who are most actively inclined pursue public office unremittingly; step by step they move through a series of positions, advancing finally to that one which either gives them satisfaction or which they are willing to tolerate, no other opportunities being available. Lest we slight the men who manifest such ambition, Joseph Schlesinger reminds us: "Representative government, above all, depends on a supply of men so driven. . . . No more irresponsible government is imaginable than one of high-minded men unconcerned for their political futures."[1]

Having previously discerned the pre-legislative careers

---

1. *Ambition and Politics: Political Careers in the United States* (Chicago: Rand McNally & Co., 1966), p. 2.

111

of New York lawmakers, we are now ready to focus upon their post-legislative careers. Here we assess the legislature as a point of embarkation and we ask: How many lawmakers go on to other positions? Who moves from this position and who does not? What are the barriers and what are the facilitations to political mobility? Of those legislators who evidence mobility, what are the typical career channels? In our attempt to treat such questions, primary attention is directed to patterns of movement. Though opportunities for office are many, political careers nevertheless tend to show certain regularities as influenced by social and political conditions. As conditions change, moreover, career patterns change as well.

One important factor which affects channels of political mobility is the political party. Voting studies indicate that most people tend to cast ballots according to the party with which they identify. "A person may have attitudes toward parties themselves; these attitudes, in turn, may condition opinions or attitudes about other subjects."[2] As a consequence, the range of public offices which are available to a politician at any point in time will vary with the electoral fortunes of the party with which he is affiliated. As there are shifts in the partisan mood of the electorate, the career potential of the politician will also vary.

But it is not only the voting returns which are the concern of the political activist; he must also be attentive to who presides over certain key offices which have wide powers of appointment. The separate party organizations seek to control a position of this kind, not only as an end in itself, but because it can serve as the key to the whole range of rewards for which politicians compete. To illustrate, the office of the President of the United States is important because of the awesome power which is latent

---

2. V. O. Key, *Public Opinion and American Democracy* (New York: Alfred A. Knopf, 1961), p. 243. See also Bernard Berelson, *et al.*, *Voting* (Chicago: The University of Chicago Press, 1954), Chap. 10.

to it. But in addition, the party which wins the Presidency can better influence membership in the Cabinet and lesser bureaucratic positions, federal judgeships and postmaster-ships, among others. Likewise, there are key positions in state government. In New York, they would include the Governor, the Comptroller, and the Attorney General. In the cities, it can generally be said that the Mayor is most important, though there usually are others depending upon the structure of the city government and its size. In a large metropolis like New York City, we would also in-clude the Controller, Borough Presidents, and the Presi-dent of the City Council.

Of additional significance is the constituency base of elected officials. Opportunities available to the city poli-tician can differ considerably from those of the rural politician. For example, a small-town legislator might have an extremely difficult time winning statewide office in an highly urbanized state and, realizing this, might not even try; a gubernatorial aspirant from a giant urban center like New York City might not be able to overcome the anti-city attitudes of voters from other parts of the state. Let us now consider these factors, and others, as they per-tain to the careers of New York lawmakers.

## POST-LEGISLATIVE POLITICAL MOBILITY

As a first step we must account for the political mo-bility of legislators subsequent to service in the lawmaking body. In an earlier chapter, we observed that, in compari-son to the Republicans, Democrats were men who were politically on the move. It was seen that they had come to the legislature at a more youthful age and therefore had more time to partake in a career. In addition, there was evidence that they were moving through the legisla-ture at a faster rate. Relative to them, the extra-legislative career potential of the Republicans was considered limited.

It is now to be seen how this appraisal has been actualized.

Table 23 shows that Republicans are indeed relatively sluggish in following a post-legislative career and that this tendency has become more pronounced over a period of time. Members of the opposition party, in contrast, have become considerably more active. In our attempt to explain this, we should recall that the Democratic party has been the traditional home of aspiring ethnic types. Such persons have always been confronted with various forms of economic discrimination. Even in New York City, the very symbol of melting-pot epithets, the banks, insurance companies, and large corporations of all types have tended to hire few of them.[3] In contrast, the open doors of the

Table 23. Number of Post-Legislative Political Positions Occupied by 1931 and 1951 Legislators.

| Number of positions | 1931 legislators | | | 1951 legislators | | |
|---|---|---|---|---|---|---|
| | Dem. | Repub. | All | Dem. | Repub. | All |
| Still in legislature* | —% | —% | —% | 14% | 3% | 8% |
| None | 52 | 61 | 57 | 35 | 68 | 54 |
| One | 31 | 28 | 29 | 47 | 24 | 33 |
| Two | 14 | 7 | 10 | 5 | 3 | 4 |
| Three | 2 | 4 | 3 | — | 2 | 1 |
| Four | 1 | 1 | 1 | — | — | — |
| Total percent | 100% | 101% | 100% | 101% | 100% | 99% |
| Total no. | 94 | 107 | 201 | 86 | 120 | 206 |

*Still in the legislature in the year 1967.

neighborhood party clubhouse have promised opportunity which many a newcomer could not easily ignore. Limited in their ability to climb the corporate ladder of success, ambitious young men with foreign names soon learned that a career in politics could also afford status and well-being. And what's more, the foreign name could serve

3. For a general treatment of this subject as it pertains to the ethnic groups of New York City, see Glazer and Moynihan.

as a lure calculated to attract votes from the immigrant-dominated constituencies. Once in public office, the average Democrat has tended to look upward and outward to other points in the political system. After all, isn't it part of the American ethos that any man can become President?

The Republicans, on the other hand, have sought power within the legislature; their majority status has encouraged this. When they became the minority party, as was the case in the Assembly from 1965 to 1968, most of the 1951 Republicans still to be found in the legislature soon packed up and retired from politics for good. But such matters will be examined more closely in the next chapter. Right now some of the more prominent patterns of extra-legislative movement must be analyzed.

## WHERE DO THEY GO IN THE FEDERAL SYSTEM?

*National recruitment*

When social and economic change laid the groundwork for Democratic victory in the presidential elections of the 1930s and 1940s, the Democratic officeholder on the lower echelons of government could anticipate new and better opportunities. As can be seen in Tables 24 and 25, members of the New York Democratic party were quite dependent upon the political "coattails" of Franklin D. Roosevelt during the fourteen years that he was President of the United States. Among the 1931 legislative personnel, more than twice as many Democrats as Republicans were recruited into the national government; and most of the former were appointed, rather than elected, to this level of public service. It was the Republicans who had to rely primarily on ballots.

Presidential assistance is not always available, however. The 1951 Republicans could not reap the same kind of rewards from a Republican President as the 1931 Demo-

Table 24. Percentage of 1931 And 1951 Legislators Recruited into Government on the National, State, County, City, and Local Levels.

| Level of government | 1931 legislators | | | 1951 legislators | | |
|---|---|---|---|---|---|---|
| | Dem. | Repub. | All | Dem. | Repub. | All |
| National | 12% | 5% | 8% | 4% | 3% | 3% |
| State | 17 | 18 | 17 | 9 | 18 | 14 |
| County | 16 | 13 | 14 | 6 | 7 | 7 |
| City | 20 | 9 | 14 | 35 | 3 | 16 |
| Local | — | 4 | 2 | — | 1 | 1 |
| None | 52 | 61 | 57 | 35 | 68 | 54 |
| Still in Legis. (1967) | — | — | — | 14 | 3 | 8 |

Note: Percentages do not add up to 100 as some legislators were recruited into more than one level of government. Legislators accounted for up to 1967.

crats did from a Democratic President. Despite the eight years of Republican leadership under Dwight D. Eisenhower (1953 to 1960), only one legislator of that party was appointed to a federal office.

We can only surmise some basic reasons for this contrast in career patterns. One consideration, as already noted, is that the Republicans tend to be older men when they reach the legislature. With youth and vigor behind them, their career potential is decidedly restricted, particularly as it might pertain to federal service. Another factor is that Roosevelt was himself a New Yorker with some substantial experience in the politics of the state, whereas Eisenhower merely assumed residency in the state when he took on the job of President of Columbia University. It is likely, therefore, that FDR was much more attuned to the patronage needs of the New York friends he left behind. In fact, when Roosevelt became President in 1933, he put James A. Farley, long-time potentate of the New York Democratic party, in charge of patronage. As reported by Bronx County leader Ed Flynn, spokesmen for

Table 25. Means of Advancement: Appointment and/or Election, 1931 and 1951 Legislators Compared.

| Level of appointive & elective positions | 1931 legislators | | | 1951 legislators | | |
|---|---|---|---|---|---|---|
| | Dem. | Repub. | All | Dem. | Repub. | All |
| National | | | | | | |
| Appointive | 7 | 2 | 9 | — | 1 | 1 |
| Elective | 4 | 3 | 7 | 3 | 2 | 5 |
| State | | | | | | |
| Appointive | 14 | 16 | 30 | 6 | 18 | 24 |
| Elective | 4 | 4 | 8 | 2 | 6 | 8 |
| County | | | | | | |
| Appointive | 11 | 9 | 20 | 1 | 3 | 4 |
| Elective | 6 | 9 | 15 | 4 | 6 | 10 |
| City | | | | | | |
| Appointive | 12 | 5 | 17 | 16 | 1 | 17 |
| Elective | 11 | 8 | 19 | 14 | 2 | 16 |
| Local | | | | | | |
| Appointive | — | — | — | — | — | — |
| Elective | — | 4 | 4 | — | 1 | 1 |
| Total | | | | | | |
| Appointive | 34 | 32 | 76 | 23 | 23 | 46 |
| Elective | 25 | 28 | 53 | 23 | 17 | 40 |

Note: Legislators are counted once, twice, three, or four times, according to the number of offices they were recruited into. Legislators accounted for up to 1967.

the state organization were well represented when federal jobs were being allocated: "With Roosevelt in the White House the new administration began to take shape. Naturally there were many discussions on the subject of patronage. In most of these meetings with the President, Farley, Howe (a New York newspaperman), and I were present."[4]

There is also some evidence that Roosevelt was much more willing to play the game of politics than was Eisenhower. While the former could be quite aggressive in the use of patronage as a technique of reward and punish-

4. *You're the Boss*, p. 144.

ment, the latter was ambivalent on such matters; and though he understood its purposes, he often deplored its uses. In his book, *Eisenhower: The Inside Story,* Robert Donovan reports that the Republican President bitterly resented what he termed "the ruthlessness of certain previous administrations" in the dispensing of spoils.[5] The author also writes of friction with New York Congressmen over the distribution of federal jobs.[6] Among others, it appears that the New York Republican legislators were made to feel the consequences of this attitude.

One final thought here is that Franklin D. Roosevelt and the New Deal heralded in a vast expansion of governmental activity on the national level. To an unprecedented degree, new agencies were created and new personnel were appointed to meet the exigencies of depression and war. During the 1950s, expansion of government did not proceed on such a grand scale and at times there were cutbacks. Thus, it can be understood that Eisenhower was not provided with comparable opportunities to make political appointments.

### State recruitment

A look at the state level shows that the political fortunes of the 1931 legislators of both parties were about the same. Approximately 17 percent of all Republicans and Democrats were recruited into state positions. One of the factors which helps explain this is that, over the succeeding years, both parties were well represented in the executive branch.[7] In the 1930s and early 1940s, Franklin D. Roosevelt and Herbert H. Lehman were Democrats who occupied the gubernatorial office. Beginning in 1943, the

5. *Eisenhower: The Inside Story* (New York: Harper and Brothers, 1956) , p. 98.

6. *Ibid.,* p. 99.

7. With few exceptions, a New York Governor is elected into office with all other statewide executive candidates of his party. There is little or no effective ticket-splitting in the election of state executives.

Republican stalwart, Thomas E. Dewey, took the ascendancy for his party and held sway until 1954. During this time, the power of appointment was used to assuage the job-seeking aspirations of the party faithful—30 out of 38 state jobs were filled through appointment.

Among the 1951 personnel we observe that the Republicans were moving into state positions twice as fast as were members of the opposition party. Again most of the advancements were through appointments. To understand why there is this variation from the earlier period, it should be remembered that in most of the years subsequent to 1951, the Republicans controlled the statehouse. Averell Harriman, a Democratic governor, managed to interrupt the reign of the Republicans for only a short period—1955 to 1959.

There is yet another explanation to the recent dearth of Democrats in state jobs. In an article on patronage in New York State, Moynihan and Wilson find that during the Harriman administration, there was considerable reluctance among Democrats to accept state offices that were beyond the confines of New York City. The trouble was that too many of them were from the city and few were likely to move to another part of the state to accept a patronage job that does not pay well.[8] This appears to be especially true of state legislators who served in the fifties.

*City recruitment*

For the Democratic members of the legislature, New York City provides the most fertile field of career opportunities. Of such persons who served in 1931, 20 percent moved into offices located in the governmental structure of that community. Among 1951 Democrats, the percentage grew to 35. This pattern of political mobility is not

---

8. Daniel P. Moynihan and James Q. Wilson, "Patronage in New York State, 1955–59," *American Political Science Review* 58 (June, 1964): 286–301.

at all unexpected, though perhaps the proportional increase is. Since the vast majority of Democratic legislators represent New York City and since this metropolis has been the traditional stronghold of the Democratic party, this is the place where they can seek various types of public offices with the most success.

To some extent, the career aspirations of Democrats were constricted when Fiorello H. La Guardia became Mayor of the City in 1933. Elected as a Republican with the support of the City Fusion party and various reform interests, he was re-elected in 1937 and 1941. In this position of leadership he could effectively control the distribution of many of the prizes of office. Also important is the fact that every time La Guardia won an election, he carried with him his running mates for Controller and President of the City Council. This was enough to guarantee control of the powerful Board of Estimate to the Republicans and their allies. It wasn't until the post-war years that Tammany mayors regained control, thus improving the fortunes of loyal Democrats.

*County recruitment*

Movement into county government comports with the generally held view that there are close ties between county politics and legislative candidates. In the more rural areas of New York State, many legislative candidates had been regularly elected from county-wide districts and had to depend, therefore, upon the county party organizations for electoral support.[9] In the highly urban areas,

---

9. The State Constitution of 1894 guaranteed at least one Assemblyman to each of the state's 62 counties (except for two which have extremely small populations). This pattern persisted until the Supreme Court ordered a new system of apportionment in 1964. In 1931, 39 Assemblymen and four Senators were elected from county-wide districts. In 1951, 45 Assemblymen and five Senators were similarly elected. It would be useful to note, furthermore, that where a Senator represents more than one county he must depend upon the chairman of his county party organization to support him when bargaining with others.

county machines like the O'Connell organization, operating in the city of Albany, and Tammany Hall of New York City have had pervasive influence over the careers of political hopefuls.

Yet if we try to discern a trend, it appears that considerably fewer personnel are moving into county government. More than anything else, this probably reflects the diminishing importance of the county as a political unit. In New York City especially, its five counties have been subject to a steady attrition of their traditional duties— all that remains of the major functionaries in each of those counties are one or two surrogate judges, a county clerk, and a district attorney. There is also a borough president for each of the five county-boroughs who serves as a chief executive and who sits on a city-wide body, the Board of Estimate. But here, the new City Charter of 1961 transferred many patronage matters out of the hands of the borough presidents to various city agencies which administer public works programs.

Legislative reapportionment, which took place in 1964, has probably also had some effect; for counties are no longer districts of representation as they previously were. It is to be expected that as a result, the long-standing connections between the counties and legislative personnel will henceforth be weaker.

### Recruitment into other local units of government

It appears that very few persons desire to hold office below the county level. If public office means money, service, and prestige, then evidently there is little of this in town, village, or school board government to entice the political activist, particularly if he had previously succeeded in reaching the state legislature. Our data show absolutely no movement of this kind among the Democrats. Of course, since most Democrats are from New York City, positions at this level are generally not available to them. Among the Republicans, however, the opportunity for grass-roots service does exist; but barely a trickle are willing to lend credence, through action, to the alleged virtues of small-town government.

## WHERE DO LEGISLATORS GO?—THE SEPARATE BRANCHES OF GOVERNMENT

After years of service in the state legislature, what public role does a person aspire to? What is he qualified to do? Table 26 provides us with some different answers for our two sample groups. If it was previously the case, in the 1930s, that the greatest number of mobile legislators found some niche for themselves in various executive agencies, a place in the judiciary has since become the prime career goal. This trend is particularly pronounced for the Democrats: close to 30 percent of those who served in 1951 have moved into judicial-type positions.[10] Furthermore, there seems to be no strong inclination towards

Table 26. Percentage of 1931 and 1951 Legislators Recruited into the Executive, Legislative and Judicial Branches of Government.

| Branch of government | 1931 legislators | | | 1951 legislators | | |
|---|---|---|---|---|---|---|
| | Dem. | Repub. | All | Dem. | Repub. | All |
| Executive | 30% | 21% | 25% | 14% | 15% | 15% |
| Legislative | 10 | 16 | 13 | 14 | 5 | 9 |
| Judicial | 13 | 8 | 10 | 28 | 12 | 18 |
| None | 52 | 61 | 57 | 35 | 68 | 54 |
| Still in legis.  (1967) | — | — | — | 14 | 3 | 8 |

Note: Percentages do not add up to 100, as some legislators were recruited into more than one branch of government. Legislators accounted for up to 1967.

10. Of the twenty-four Democrats recruited into the judicial branch, 23 were judges and only one worked in the capacity of a clerk. Twenty-three of the twenty-four judges acquired their positions in the New York City judicial system.

other kinds of legislative office, as might be presupposed.

For an overall picture of recruitment patterns, let us focus on Table 27 where there is outlined a more detailed distribution of offices into which the lawmakers were channeled. Those legislators who show no post-legislative mobility are not considered here.

## Legislative recruitment

Contrary to expectations, legislators are not likely to use their lawmaking experience once they move on to other governmental offices. Nor does there seem to be any special career link with Congress. Instead, the trend has been toward movement into the other two branches of government wherein they perform functions for which they are not necessarily prepared. In this respect, state legislative service appears to be a kind of political apprenticeship. It is the development of political skills and qualities, e.g., verbal ability, adroitness at bargaining, and "loyalty" to the powers that be, which is probably stressed more than anything else. This is the way legislators prove their worth for a better job, wherever it may be.

In a sense, also, the legislature can be seen as the place where eligibility is established for other, usually more lucrative positions in the political system. Such eligibility is often determined by the personal characteristics of lawmakers as they fit special circumstances. For example, factional or regional affiliations may be the basis for advancement, particularly if some appointing authority, say the Governor, feels compelled to distribute such rewards as the price of getting his program through the legislature. In addition, promotion of legislators may be based on the necessity of granting "recognition" to certain groups in the community, especially ethnic and religious groups. Note the "qualifications" for prospective appointees to the fifteen-member State Board of Social Welfare as specified in a letter to Governor Harriman:

Table 27. Percentage Distribution of Types of Governmental Positions into which 1931 and 1951 Legislators Were Recruited.

| Type of governmental office | 1931 legislators | | | 1951 legislators | | |
|---|---|---|---|---|---|---|
| | Dem. | Repub. | All | Dem. | Repub. | All |
| **Executive** | | | | | | |
| National | 10% | 2% | 6% | —% | —% | —% |
| State | 16 | 14 | 15 | 6 | 33 | 18 |
| County | 21 | 17 | 19 | 9 | 8 | 8 |
| City | 10 | 16 | 13 | 10 | 5 | 8 |
| Local | — | 4 | 2 | — | 3 | 1 |
| Total | 57 | 53 | 55 | 25 | 49 | 35 |
| **Legislative** | | | | | | |
| National | 6 | 5 | 6 | 6 | 5 | 6 |
| State | 3 | 14 | 8 | 6 | 5 | 6 |
| County | — | 5 | 3 | — | 3 | 1 |
| City | 5 | 4 | 4 | 13 | — | 7 |
| Local | — | 4 | 2 | — | — | — |
| Total | 14 | 32 | 23 | 25 | 13 | 20 |
| **Judicial** | | | | | | |
| National | 2 | 2 | 2 | — | 3 | 1 |
| State | 8 | 5 | 6 | 4 | 20 | 12 |
| County | 3 | 4 | 3 | 2 | 13 | 7 |
| City | 16 | 3 | 10 | 44 | 3 | 25 |
| Local | — | 2 | 1 | — | — | — |
| Total | 29 | 16 | 22 | 50 | 39 | 45 |
| **All branches** | | | | | | |
| National | 18 | 9 | 14 | 6 | 8 | 7 |
| State | 27 | 33 | 29 | 17 | 59 | 36 |
| County | 24 | 26 | 25 | 10 | 23 | 16 |
| City | 31 | 23 | 27 | 67 | 8 | 40 |
| Local | — | 10 | 5 | — | 3 | 1 |
| Total | 100% | 101% | 100% | 100% | 101% | 100% |

Note: Legislators evidencing no mobility are not considered here. Recruitment is accounted for up to 1967.

There are longstanding traditions as to the composition of the membership of the Board. For instance, the members are divided religiously as follows: 7 Protestants, 5 Catholics, 3 Jews. There is always one Negro member of the Board. It is customary to have 10 men and five women on the Board. There has been a longstanding custom of having two doctors on the Board. . . .[11]

The problem posed in such a situation is that competence in government must compete with the need to consolidate power and reward the faithful. The problem grows more acute, we might add, the poorer the quality of personnel recruited into politics.

## Executive recruitment

Our data reveals that more than half of all 1931 mobile legislators moved into executive posts. In addition, we see that members of both parties were almost evenly matched in their use of this channel of advancement. After 1951, however, it is evident that only the Republicans have continued to rely heavily on executive promotions, especially on the state level; it is here more than anywhere else that they have become entrenched.

A dilemma which confronts any Republican Governor, then, is deciding where to place members of the legislature when expectations of appointive reward cannot be denied. What is perhaps unavoidable is that some state agencies get more of their share of such appointments than others, thus serving, in effect, as retiring grounds for old political war-horses. The following editorial is typical of the kind of complaints which this situation instigates:

In his years at Albany Governor Rockefeller has made many excellent appointments to public office. His talent for picking good men, however, has never been applied to

11. The letter was sent by the Department of Social Welfare. Quoted in Moynihan and Wilson, pp. 297–98.

the Public Service Commission. . . . The fact that its administration has been under constant criticism stems from the long and unfortunate tradition of staffing the commission with ex-politicians. Unaccountably, Mr. Rockefeller has gone along with this practice, choosing men whose only apparent qualifications have been their loyal and lengthy service in Republican ranks.[12]

We should note that a substantial proportion of the "ex-politicians" referred to formerly served in the legislature.

To the extent that Democrats rely on positions in administrative agencies, it is New York City and the five counties within the city that afford the greatest opportunity. In the dispensing of city jobs, the Mayor is most important and can thereby compete with the Governor as a political force, particularly if they both belong to the Democratic party. Big-city Democrats, after all, find many metropolitan posts just as enticing as state jobs, sometimes more so because of their more suitable location. The availability of such patronage can also work as a source of leverage, helping to assure legislative consideration of the city's needs—though this is not to say that it would assure the provision of these needs. It is probably in the area of judicial appointments, however, that the Mayor can play a stronger role; for as we shall see shortly, such positions are more actively sought after by those who play the game of politics.[13]

## Judicial recruitment

In the spring of 1962, the Democratic party was obviously having a great deal of difficulty finding qualified candidates for nomination to two important statewide elective posts: Governor and United States Senator. In partial explanation of why this was so, one veteran observer of the state's politics wrote a journalistic article with

---

12. The *New York Times,* March 25, 1967.
13. In New York City, judges for the Criminal and Family Courts are appointed by the Mayor.

the following headline: "Vanishing Candidates—Many Promising Democrats Have Fled Turmoil of Politics for Quiet of Bench."[14] In this special way, the judiciary makes its impact on New York politics.

The information in Table 27 seems to vindicate this contention. Apparently, though, the 1931 legislators were not as yet able to take full advantage of this career channel as less than a fourth of those who were mobile came to occupy judicial posts. After 1951, however, we see a drastic shift in career patterns. Half of all mobile Democrats had advanced into the judiciary and 44 percent of them had attained such offices in New York City alone. Nor are the Republicans far behind, though they depend primarily on the state and counties for such promotions.

How do we account for this lure of the bench? The answer lies in a composite of many things. One is the search for economic well-being. Judicial salaries in New York are among the highest in the nation, on occasion even exceeding those on the United States Supreme Court. Another is the prestige of high social status which accrues to the office, a quality which is particularly appealing to the social climbers. A third is the escape it offers from the disillusionment and turmoil of politics. "Talented young Democratic legislators often get the feeling that they are only errand boys for political leaders, with little opportunity to show initiative and judgment."[15]

Of course, judicial recruitment would not be nearly so prominent if the lawmakers did not have the requisite legal training. We shall consider this interrelationship of lawyer, legislator, and judge in a later chapter.

## THE BIPOLARIZATION OF POLITICAL CAREERS

Overall, Table 27 shows a fairly even distribution of 1931 legislators moving into the various levels of govern-

---

14. Leo Eagan, The *New York Times,* June 4, 1962.
15. *Ibid.*

ment.[16] The chief reason for this is that, with the exception of the national government, no one party fully dominated any one governmental area during the 1930s and 1940s. However, in the years subsequent to 1951 we have a case of another kind. The trend has been toward a bipolarization of political careers.

In New York State, Democratic lawmakers aim their sights toward New York City offices where Democratic electoral majorities make success highly probable. They no longer appear very willing or capable of achieving state positions. Since the Republicans have come to dominate the state's administrative machinery, including the governorship, legislators of this party can depend upon state executive appointments as an important means of advancement. At the same time, they show little or no experience in New York's largest urban center. Thus two broadly different career perspectives have evolved within the legislature which correspond to the basic partisan division of the institution. Because of their determination to follow the same well-grooved career paths as the surest means to political survival, legislator-politicians often lack the skill and capacity to lead on a statewide basis—few men can bridge the gap between metropolitan and upstate electorates. This is why only three lawmakers (two Republicans in 1931 and one Republican in 1951) out of a total of over four hundred in our sample sessions were ever elected to statewide office. While many have tried, the last time a former legislator achieved the office of Governor of New York was when Franklin D. Roosevelt won the post in 1928 and again in 1930.[17] Nor is it the case that United States Senators indicate state legislative experience

16. See the bottom of Table 27.

17. In his book, *How They Became Governor* (East Lansing: Michigan State University, 1957), Joseph A. Schlesinger explains that "the state legislature is most likely to lead to the governorship when the electorates for the two offices are most similar. . . . Urbanism has reduced the homogeneity of interests. Hence the legislature has dropped in importance as a route to the governor." P. 48.

as in former times. The last one with such credentials was Irving M. Ives who ran successful campaigns in 1946 and in 1952.

This illustrates one of the principal inadequacies of the New York legislative parties. In the words of V. O. Key: "Perhaps the most important function that party leadership needs to perform is the development, grooming, and promotion of candidates for statewide office. . . . It is in its inadequacy in this role that the most grave shortcoming of party leadership is to be found."[18]

## TYPES OF CAREERS

In attempting to generalize about political careers, the thoughts of Max Weber, the noted German sociologist, are most suggestive. He states that there are basically two types of politicians: one who lives "for" politics and one who lives "off" politics. "He who strives to make politics a permanent source of income lives 'off' politics as a vocation, whereas he who does not do this lives 'for' politics."[19] In the latter case, the man is motivated "by the consciousness that his life has meaning in the service of a 'cause.'" Economic gain is of secondary or no importance to him. In the former case, "political leadership is made accessible to propertyless men who must then be rewarded."[20] That is to say, men of this kind are more disposed toward using politics as a means to private advantage. Weber acknowledges, furthermore, that the distinction between the two types is not an exclusive one as there is usually at least some overlap in their motivations, i.e., those who live "for" politics can and do seek personal gain and those who live "off" politics generally have some ideological concerns.

18. V. O. Key, *American State Politics*, p. 271.
19. In H. H. Gerth and C. Wright Mills (eds.) , *From Max Weber: Essays in Sociology*, pp. 84–85.
20. *Ibid.*

Such classification, when modified, can be readily applied to an analysis of New York legislators. Here we try to gauge the life styles of politicians using the criteria of (1) social origins and (2) length and nature of public service. Knowledge of social origins provides us with a useful clue into the motives of individuals. If someone is derived from fairly high social status and then becomes politically active while maintaining his status, he is less likely to be preoccupied with the use of politics primarily for material well-being. A person who rises from the lower levels of society usually has no choice in the matter, especially in the early stages of his career. As for the second criterion, by scrutinizing the length and nature of public service, we can assess, to some degree, his commitment to public duty. For example, an emphasis on low-paying local office, either before or after his legislative tour, would indicate a "service" perspective; an emphasis on post-legislative office of high repute would reflect a "career" perspective. In all, three basic categories are set up as follows. (See data in Tables 28 and 29.)

## Patron-Politicians

Reference is to those who stress support and protection of the older, more traditional values of society. Here there is preoccupation with the gilded heritage of communal life as it was or "should be": neighborliness, moral rectitude, and honest industry are some of the more prominent values subscribed to. Patrons believe that such qualities can be used to defend against the crass ingredients of mass-industrial society, or that they can be counted on as guidelines for leadership in the face of changing conditions.

Here, too, can be found the special defenders of democracy. "The American tradition of democracy was formed on the farm and in small villages, and its central ideas were founded in rural sentiments and on rural metaphors (we still speak of 'grass-roots democracy'). . . . A certain complacency and self-righteousness thus entered into rural thinking, and this complacency was rudely shocked by the conquests of industrialism."[21] The ideological ves-

Table 28. Political Party and Types of Careers, 1931 and 1951.

| Types of Careers | 1931 legislators | | | 1951 legislators | | |
|---|---|---|---|---|---|---|
| | Dem. | Repub. | All | Dem. | Repub. | All |
| Careerists | 76% | 29% | 51% (N 103) | 80% | 36% | 54% (N 112) |
| Patrons | 11% | 61% | 38% (N 75) | 12% | 59% | 39% (N 81) |
| Amateurs | 13% | 10% | 11% (N 23) | 8% | 5% | 6% (N 13) |
| Total percent | 100% | 100% | 100% (N 201) | 100% | 100% | 99% (N 206) |

tiges of such ideas still persist and, indeed, there appears to be a concerted effort by many a lawmaker to project an image of the yeoman-farmer even when heavily implicated in the more typical forms of contemporary employment.[22]

Persons who approximate such faith are the very foundation of Republican membership. They consist primarily of old-stock businessmen, farmers, and professional men from the smaller cities and towns. Among them also, epitomizing the classical ideals of *noblesse oblige,* can be found a scattering of patricians—i.e., persons derived from the oldest families in the state and nation and who represent status and wealth; their numbers, we might note, continue to diminish. All together, the Patrons endorse a program of low taxes, a balanced budget and minimal govern-

21. Richard Hofstadter, *The Age of Reform,* p. 7.
22. Of all those who claimed to be engaged in agriculture in the 1931 session, 59 percent were engaged in other occupational and business activities. The same was true of 22 percent of the 1951 legislators.

Table 29. Profile of Careerists, Patrons, and Amateurs, 1931 and 1951.

| | 1931 legislators | | | 1951 legislators | | |
|---|---|---|---|---|---|---|
| | C | P | A | C | P | A |
| | (N 103) | (N 75) | (N 23) | (N 112) | (N 81) | (N 13) |
| Pre-legislative experience | 31% | 63% | 17% | 45% | 67% | 23% |
| Post-legislative experience* | 64% | 29% | 9% | 61% | 14% | — |
| Tenure—less than 16 yrs. in legis. | 83% | 69% | 100% | 60% | 41% | 100% |
| Age when elected to legis. —under 40 yrs. | 70% | 37% | 30% | 54% | 26% | 46% |
| Ethnic background† | 68% | 8% | 39% | 78% | 21% | 69% |
| New York City residency | 62% | 13% | 48% | 66% | 12% | 61% |
| Occupation | | | | | | |
| Business managerial | 27% | 29% | 39% | 22% | 41% | 8% |
| Lawyers | 53% | 35% | 43% | 65% | 39% | 61% |
| Other professional & technical | 7% | 13% | — | 4% | 11% | 15% |
| Farmers | 4% | 21% | 9% | 1% | 9% | 8% |
| Salaried workers & wage earners | 9% | 1% | 9% | 8% | — | 8% |

* Accounted for up to 1967.
† Reference is to Irish, Jews, Italians, Negroes, Poles and Germans.

mental activity. This was especially the case in the 1930s and the following excerpts from the letter of a complaining Republican Assemblyman serve as useful illustration:

> I introduced the gasolene tax bill, the state road bill and bridge bill as well as maintenance bill to make state roads a state wide proposition, yet there was no action and no co-operation from those who should have seen the hand writing on the wall. . . .
> The so called leaders were so put out with me that they

somewhat ludicrous, to say the least, they nevertheless reflect the persisting temper of what are mostly New York City, ethnic-stock individuals who have long dominated the Democratic party. It was the Irish who first set the tone, bringing to the party system a strong sense of hierarchy and an elaborate bureaucracy. Seniority rather than sheer ability became the prime criterion for political advancement and everyone learned to wait his turn. "Instead of letting politics transform them," writes Glazer and Moynihan, "the Irish transformed politics, establishing a political system in New York City that, from a distance, seems like the social system of an Irish village writ large."[27] Thus saddled by concepts of structure, the party organization has always found it difficult to perceive, no less treat, new and mounting problems of twentieth-century urban America. The Irish "never thought of politics as an instrument of social change—their kind of politics involved the processes of a society that was not changing."[28]

This, then, has been the inheritance of New York City democracy. Even as the Jews and Italians found their way in and began to take control, the established pattern continued: "At the rough-neck clubhouse level [the party] has hardly changed in the thirty years since Jim Farley, that big, pink, laughing man, ran it from the high-domed office of the Postmaster General in Washington. It is a system of regional satrapies and political clubhouses almost guaranteed to produce political hacks."[29] Whenever possible, the party pays homage to the tried and true programs of Franklin D. Roosevelt's New Deal—it helps capture the urban vote. The membership favors labor power over the corporations and the ethnic underdog over the Yankee mugwump. But even in these areas, Negroes and Puerto Ricans complain of major oversights and hypocrisy.

27. *Beyond the Melting Pot,* p. 226.
28. *Ibid.,* p. 229.
29. Richard Armstrong. "Bobby Kennedy and the Fight for New York," *The Saturday Evening Post,* November 6, 1965, p. 87.

Recently arrived on the political scene is a new group of politicians who, in perspective and style, represent a threat to the established elements of both major parties. They can be called the "new breed." Evidencing professional and managerial skills, such persons are usually third or fourth generation ethnics or of Yankee background. Among the Democrats, this type consists for the most part of young lawyers and junior executives who are located in New York City. Most significant, in distinguishing them from the old-timers, is that they have generally managed to achieve cultural assimilation to the point where old ethnic ties and concern for ethnic recognition are no longer of paramount importance. While their interest in jobs and status persists, they are also secure enough, economically, to stress broad community goals, e.g., parks, schools, and redevelopment. Manifest, also, is a strong-felt intolerance of civic corruption. Reform-oriented, they seek to democratize party methods by purging the organization of "bossism." In a few instances, such insurgents have found their way to the legislature where they exude an air of independence and a zeal for polemics.

But here, too, we find careerists, though with a greater show of idealism. James Q. Wilson reminds us that party reform has provided greater opportunities for ambitious young politicians by giving them a base of power from which they can negotiate on behalf of their political careers. "In the past, rising in the party bureaucracy was painfully slow for the young lawyer; reformism can make that rise very rapid indeed."[30] The one major consequence of the reform movement, so far, has been factional struggle; as yet, new ideas and new talents have not been crystallized in any meaningful way.

The Republicans are also experiencing an increase in career politicians, but here there appears to be greater recruitment of the "new breed" type. Instrumental in

30. *The Amateur Democrat*, pp. 139–140.

effecting this has been the rapid growth of the suburbs, centers of Republican strength in almost all parts of New York. Such places are producing a new middle-class grouping of upward aspiring "organization men." Because they are highly mobile, geographically as well as socially, this type reveals a more permissive attitude toward governmental activity than has been true of the more stable Patrons. While in agreement with the latter on the need to preserve traditional community forms (e.g., small government is to be preferred to big government), their concern also focuses upon the urgency of environmental problems; particularly as it affects them in the areas of transportation, education and recreation. Status-oriented, suburban politicians view legislative office as the means of achieving greater influence among business and social compatriots; for local officials and interest groups must come to them to get the state laws they need. Where such politicians are lawyers, and many of them are, new contacts with clientele groups are assured. As legislative reapportionment on the basis of "one man, one vote" takes effect and the suburbs continue to grow, this kind of careerist is likely to assume dominance in the Republican party. Thus they represent a new and rising threat to the old Patron hegemony.

## Amateur Politicians

Politicians in this category are distinguished by their low degree of political involvement as measured by the fact that they have served less than a total of ten years in public office. Most significant, from our data, is the very low proportion of such persons in the legislature and the fact that they have decreased from eleven percent to six percent over the twenty-year period surveyed.

Formerly, a goodly proportion of them were of the business-executive class and could be found as much in the upstate areas as in New York City. More recently, however, they appear to be concentrated in the metropolis and are largely members of the legal profession. Thus, we see a shifting away in this category from the old mugwump or dilettante type, one who condescended to politics, to the urban rebel type. As Wilson describes him, this is a new kind of politician who shows distrust of both professional politicians and big businessmen. Young, cosmopolitan and middle-class, he "sees the political world more in terms of ideas and principles than in terms of persons. Politics is the determination of public policy, and public policy ought to be set deliberately rather than as the accidental by-product of a struggle for personal and party advantage."[31]

What happens to such persons? Many of the more ambitious ones come to place less stress on ideals as they develop career stakes of their own; as such, they move into the careerist category. Some drop out, having other things to do. And still others, given their low-skill, amateur orientation, simply cannot survive in a state where politics is highly professionalized.

31. *Ibid.*, p. 3.

# 7

# LAWYER-LEGISLATORS AND THE PURSUIT OF JUDGESHIPS

A number of contemporary studies have revealed what appears to be a natural affinity between lawyers and American politics.[1] No other occupational group evidences a greater and more persisting involvement in political affairs than do members of the legal profession. As Heinz Eulau and John D. Sprague phrase it: "In the United States, probably more than in any other nation, lawyers are the 'high priests of politics.' "[2]

Though there has been considerable speculation as to the factors which contribute to this phenomenon, many prevailing assumptions are yet to be tested under empirical conditions. One typical explanation emphasizes the advantages that the lawyer enjoys in politics which sets him apart from persons in other occupations. For example, he can project a more favorable image of himself as an attorney when he also assumes the role of representative of the people. Through public acquaintance with other

---

1. Joseph A. Schlesinger, "Lawyers and American Politics: A Clarified View," *Midwest Journal of Political Science* 1 (May, 1957) : 28; David R. Derge, "The Lawyer in the Indiana General Assembly," *Midwest Journal of Political Science* 6 (February, 1962) : 21; Donald R. Matthews, *U.S. Senators and Their World* (Chapel Hill: University of North Carolina Press, 1960) , pp. 33–36; Donald R. Matthews, *The Social Background of Political Decision-Makers* (New York: Random House, 1954) , p. 30.
2. *Lawyers in Politics* (New York: Bobbs-Merrill, 1964) , p. 11.

lawyers and private groups he stands to gain a large clientele for his legal services. In addition, it is explained that the attorney's trade is flexible and less likely to be upset by the uncertainties which are inherent in politics.

Our basic premise is that the political prominence of attorneys in the legislature and in the State of New York can, to a significant extent, be attributed to the large urban community. Here can be found that combination of cultural and political factors which tends to promote the political careers of lawyers more than other occupational groups. The existence of a great metropolis like New York City in the state seemingly provides the right opportunity to test the proposition.

## LAWYERS AS CAREER POLITICIANS

A necessary first step is to assess the lawyer's commitment to politics. One general assumption is that the legal practitioner is strongly motivated to pursue a public career and is more active, politically, than are persons of other occupations. He tends to enter politics at an earlier age and goes further in the government hierarchy than, say, the businessman or journalist. In this respect, the lawyer-politician is considered a "careerist."

The data from our two sample sessions seem to support this view (see Table 30). Not only do members of the bar enter the legislature at a more youthful age than do non-lawyers, but a higher percentage of them begin legislative service with no prior governmental experience. Apparently, the legislator who is a barrister is better able to jump directly into government on a fairly high level, thus getting a head start on his fellow representatives.

At least two reasons can be suggested which may account for this. First, the legal experience of lawyers of itself can be considered a kind of political apprenticeship. In the practice of their profession, they develop certain qualities and skills which stand them in good stead as both politicians and legislators, e.g., knowledge of the law, verbal skills. Second, it may be the case that attorneys, strongly attracted to a political career, are more systematic and purposeful in their approach. Accordingly, they press for a "quick start" and deliberately begin their careers as high up on the governmental ladder as possible. Further insight into this matter will be afforded later in the chapter.

Table 30. Lawyers Compared with Nonlawyers by Selected Characteristics, 1931 and 1951.

| Characteristics | Lawyers | | Nonlawyers | |
|---|---|---|---|---|
| | 1931 | 1951 | 1931 | 1951 |
| Age upon entrance into the legislature: less than 35 years | 62% | 34% | 26% | 14% |
| Prior governmental experience | 32% | 48% | 49% | 60% |
| Legislative tenure: more than sixteen sessions* | 4% | 26% | 15% | 37% |
| Post-legislative political mobility† | 55% | 50% | 35% | 25% |
| Total number | 91 | 113 | 108 | 93 |

\* Tenure is accounted for up to the 1967 session. Members of the Assembly were elected for one year terms until 1938 when, in accordance with a constitutional amendment, the term was extended to two years.

† Movement of legislators into other governmental positions is accounted for up to 1967.

Of additional significance is the fact that lawyers move through the legislature at a more rapid rate than do others. There is good cause for this: they have greater opportunity, and apparently the desire as well, to establish themselves elsewhere in the political system. Note, in Table 30, the comparatively high percentage of attorneys who move into other public office subsequent to legislative service. In all, the evidence tends to confirm the proposition that lawyer-politicians not only *serve* in the legislature, but they *use* it as well. For many such persons, the lawmaking body is a way station or steppingstone to more desirable positions in the governmental arena.

## LAWYERS AND LAW-ENFORCEMENT OFFICE

Given his earlier start in the legislature and greater propensity for advancement, the lawyer seems to be firmly rooted in the politics of New York. Among the various explanations for such findings in other political structures, Joseph Schlesinger's are most suggestive. In his study of the careers of American governors, he finds that: "The lawyer's advantage in politics derives not so much from generalized political skills as from specific legal skills which give him a monopoly of office related to the administration of law in the court system."[3] From general knowledge, it would seem that this observation could have reference to the New York lawyer.

### Law-enforcement experience

The task at hand is to test our supposition in the light of available evidence. We must discern the extent to which the lawyer-legislators in our two samples depend upon law-enforcement positions as a means of initiating their political careers. For the year 1931, Table 31 shows that in those cases where attorneys indicated prior governmental experience, more than half of them had participated in public service related to the administration of law in the court system. But by 1951, this characteristic had become more pronounced. Of the 54 lawyers who had previously served in government, three-fourths of them manifested law-enforcement experience.

This process can be illustrated by the Corporation Counsel's office in New York City which provides a special niche for politically inspired attorneys. This is the agency which handles the legal business of the city government. Sayre and Kaufman discuss one of its important

---

3. "Lawyers and American Politics: A Clarified View," pp. 26–27.

Table 31. Law-Enforcement Experience: Lawyers and Nonlawyers Compared, 1931 and 1951.

| Type of governmental experience | Lawyers | | Nonlawyers | |
|---|---|---|---|---|
| | 1931 | 1951 | 1931 | 1951 |
| Law-enforcement experience* | 53% | 76% | 11% | 5% |
| Other governmental experience | 47% | 24% | 89% | 95% |
| Total percent | 100% | 100% | 100% | 100% |
| Total number | 30 | 54 | 53 | 56 |

NOTE: The figures are a percentage of all those who evidenced prior governmental experience. Those without experience are not included.

* Law-enforcement experience refers to governmental positions related to the administration of the law in the courts. Essentially, this includes judicial and public attorney offices.

functions: "The Corporation Counsel heads a large staff of lawyers, perhaps justifiably described as 'the largest legal firm in the city,' thus holding at his disposal several hundred choice assignments for members of a profession that have a unique intimacy with, and special skills in, the political process. These staff members . . . tend to have strong career aspirations in politics. . . ."[4]

Throughout the state, lawyers can begin a political career as a United States attorney, an assistant state attorney general, a district attorney, a governmental counsel, or a judge among other positions. Another related inducement for political involvement, which is not revealed by our statistics, are the many appointments as referees, guardians and executors of estates which are available only to lawyers. Usually it is "connections" through the party organization that make such prizes, as well as other benefits, available to them. A former lawyer-legislator expounds:

Politics is supposed to be the calling of lawyers, and young lawyers join [party] clubs because many of the jobs that are available are for lawyers. And, in addition to that,

4. *Governing New York City*, p. 358.

the lawyers join clubs because they believe they can expand their contacts, perhaps get to meet judges at campaign time. They don't want to be strangers in Courts.[5]

## Law-enforcement mobility

According to our scheme, we must also determine the degree to which lawyers rely upon public attorney positions and judgeships as a means of post-legislative advancement. Again, we may note in Table 32 the increasing

Table 32. Percentage of Mobile Lawyers Recruited in Law-Enforcement and Other Governmental Office, 1931 and 1951.

| Type of governmental office | Lawyers | |
|---|---|---|
| | 1931 | 1951 |
| Law-enforcement | | |
|   Judicial office | 33% | 69% |
|   Government attorney | 19% | 7% |
|   Total percent | 52% | 76% |
| | N 27 | N 42 |
| Other governmental office | 48% | 24% |
| | N 25 | N 13 |

NOTE: Political mobility is accounted for up to 1967. Recruitment of mobile nonlawyers is not considered here because their movement into law-enforcement office is almost nonexistent.

trend toward dependence on these types of offices. It appears that the desire for judicial office is of special significance here. About one-third of all positions filled by 1931 lawyers were in the judiciary. Among the 1951 lawyers, the proportion has grown to more than two-thirds. Over the same period of time, government attorney positions seem to have become less alluring, as indicated by a drop from nineteen percent to eight percent.[6]

5. Ludwig Teller, p. 86.
6. Table 32 does not account for the law-enforcement mobility of nonlawyers because there is almost no indication of such a pattern.

Why is the judgeship such an enticement? Sayre and Kaufman explain:

> Even the most prominent lawyers appearing before the most obscure judges cannot escape the fact that the latter are their superiors in the courtroom. And the habits—indeed, the obligations—of deference accorded by tradition to those who sit in the highest positions in an old and esteemed profession carry over; in court and out, judges are automatically part of the legal elite, and it is not surprising that so many lawyers yearn to sit on the bench. The sense of the majesty of the law and of the judges who represent it is even more impressive to the laymen involved in judicial proceedings, even for nothing more important than traffic violations; the robes, the formalities, the authority of these men elevate them to something apart from ordinary beings. Judges, like physicians, are surrounded by an honorific aura that to many is both awesome and wonderful.[7]

Material rewards are also abundant. Judges are the most highly paid among governmental officials and, in New York, their salaries sometimes exceed those paid to United States Supreme Court Justices. Working conditions are usually pleasant and terms of office are long. This growing link between legislature and judiciary may be a key factor in accounting for the expanding proportion of lawyers entering New York legislative politics; for the opportunity to don the cloak of judicial respectability is restricted almost entirely to members of the legal profession.

## THE URBAN BASIS TO THE DOMINANCE OF LAWYERS

We have demonstrated how lawyers in the New York legislature have become quite dependent upon law-enforcement jobs as a means of initiating and perpetuating their political careers. It follows, therefore, that lawyer-

---

7. P. 531.

politicians will tend to be more heavily concentrated in those places where politics is closely intertwined with the legal processes of the courts.[8]

Table 33 presents a classification of legislators' districts according to their urban-rural character.[9] It can be seen here that about 60 percent of all lawyer-legislators who served in 1931 and 1951 came from New York City. In

Table 33. Distribution of Lawyers and Nonlawyers According to Type of District, 1931 and 1951.

| Type of district | Lawyers | | Nonlawyers | |
|---|---|---|---|---|
| | 1931 | 1951 | 1931 | 1951 |
| New York City | 60% | 61% | 27% | 25% |
| | N 56 | N 69 | N 29 | N 23 |
| 100,000+ | 14% | 10% | 12% | 13% |
| | N 13 | N 11 | N 13 | N 12 |
| 25,000+ | 5% | 8% | 13% | 9% |
| | N 5 | N 9 | N 14 | N 8 |
| 2,500+ | 9% | 11% | 12% | 18% |
| | N 8 | N 12 | N 13 | N 17 |
| −2,500 | 12% | 11% | 36% | 35% |
| | N 11 | N 12 | N 39 | N 33 |
| Total percent | 100% | 101% | 100% | 100% |
| Total number | 93 | 113 | 108 | 93 |

contrast, those of other occupations are more evenly distributed along the continuum. According to our hypothesis, then, this pattern should be a manifestation of a more intensive political involvement of the courts in New York City than elsewhere in the state. One way of measuring this is to relate the law-enforcement experience of legislators to the urban-rural scale.

8. In his study of American governors, Joseph A. Schlesinger traces regional differences in the dominance of lawyers across the nation.
9. See Chapter 2, note 4, *supra*.

*Type of district and law-enforcement experience*

Interestingly enough, Table 34 indicates that the highest percentage of those 1931 legislators whose background includes law-enforcement activity represented the most rural districts. This is contrary to expectations. When it is considered, however, that justice of the peace and police justice offices prevail in the towns and villages, the finding can be easily understood; for these are usually part-time, elective jobs which need not be filled by attorneys. In our

Table 34. Law-Enforcement Characteristics of Legislators According to Type of District, 1931 and 1951.

| Type of district | 1931 legislators | | | 1951 legislators | | |
|---|---|---|---|---|---|---|
| | N | | % | N | | % |
| Law-enforcement experience | | | | | | |
| New York City | 5 | | 23 | 19 | | 43 |
| 100,000+ | 2 | | 9 | 5 | ( 2 judges) | 12 |
| 25,000+ | 3 | ( 2 judges) | 14 | 4 | ( 2 judges) | 9 |
| 2,500+ | 2 | | 9 | 7 | ( 5 judges) | 16 |
| −2,500 | 10 | ( 6 judges) | 45 | 9 | ( 6 judges) | 20 |
| Total | 22 | ( 8 judges) | 100 | 44 | (15 judges) | 100 |
| Advancement into law-enforcement Office* | | | | | | |
| New York City | 17 | (13 judges) | 63 | 30 | (26 judges) | 71 |
| 100,000+ | 1 | ( 1 judge ) | 4 | 4 | ( 4 judges) | 10 |
| 25,000+ | 2 | ( 1 judge ) | 7 | 2 | ( 2 judges) | 5 |
| 2,500+ | 1 | | 4 | 4 | ( 4 judges) | 10 |
| −2,500 | 6 | ( 2 judges) | 22 | 2 | ( 2 judges) | 5 |
| Total | 27 | (17 judges) | 100 | 42 | (38 judges) | 101 |

* Political advancement is accounted for up to 1967.

1931 sample, 8 of 17 law-enforcement positions outside New York City were so occupied. The significance of this is that the upstate lawyers were not provided with much of an advantage here. If a monopoly, or near monopoly, of court-related offices does not exist, then a dominance of lawyers cannot be expected. Within New York City, however, only attorneys are legally eligible for such positions. Hence we can account for the heavy concentration of lawyers from the big city. (At this initial stage in their careers, all New York City barristers served as public attorneys rather than as judges.)

The 1951 legislators can be analyzed in much the same way. Numerically, the rural lawmakers were as well represented as formerly. Again the principal resource was the local judiciary—with or without lawyer eligibility. But during this later period it appears that a new recruitment pattern developed. Almost four times as many New York City lawyers took advantage of their special kind of job monopoly (all served in public attorney positions). Accordingly, the percentage distribution of legislators with law-enforcement experience is now decidedly weighted toward the metropolis. How can we explain such change?

## New York City legislators: a tale of lawyers and judgeships

It can be argued that as the politics of the city comes to provide more and better rewards which are of a legal nature, the metropolitan attorney tries harder than ever to get a start somewhere, anywhere in the governmental structure. This is borne out by our data in Table 34 which shows New York City accounting for a growing proportion of all such post-legislative positions. Most significant here is the role of the judgeship as a symbol of prestige and achievement. As previously described, positions of this kind are eagerly sought after by members of the bar; and, indeed, the political leaders distribute such jobs with considerable discernment, usually as reward for faithful party service. But the question which we must consider is: why is this condition more relevant to New York City than it is to the rest of the state?

Part of the answer is that New York City judgeships are generally more highly regarded than are similar positions elsewhere in the state. While there are only about 380 judicial posts available in New York City[10] as compared to about 3,000 upstate,[11] judgeships in the metropolis are higher-paying, full-time responsibilities. It is understandable that such office should have greater prestige than the low-paying often part-time judicial posts which abound in other areas. Even State Supreme Court justices who function in New York City draw more in salary than do their counterparts in upstate New York.[12]

In addition, reference must be made to the social origins of big-city lawyers. The available information reveals a significantly greater proportion of New York City lawyers, as compared to those from upstate, who are derived from low status, foreign-stock families (Table 35). Most of them attended law schools part-time in the evening— a scheme which permits opportunity for self-supporting employment.[13] Though aspiring to "higher" positions in society, persons of such backgrounds have been limited in their ability to take advantage of the traditional channels of social mobility. Initially lacking resources and generally excluded from the corporate world of business and finance, the Irish, Jews, and Italians have had to take whatever opportunities were available. One such opportunity has been a career in politics. In a polyglot city like

10. This is estimated by Sayre and Kaufman, p. 526.

11. This estimate is derived from *A Guide to Court Systems* (New York: Institute of Judicial Administration, 1960) and *The New York Red Book, 1960–61* (Albany: Williams Press, 1960), pp. 297–318.

12. To illustrate, in 1960, Supreme Court justices in the metropolis received $34,500 a year. Upstate they received $29,000. The difference in salary was, and still is, paid by New York City. See *A Guide to Court Systems, ibid.,* p. 28.

13. Law schools are rated according to a scheme outlined in Chap. 3.

Table 35. Social Origins: New York City Lawyers Compared with Upstate Lawyers, 1931 and 1951.

| | NYC Lawyers | | Upstate lawyers | |
|---|---|---|---|---|
| Characteristics | 1931 | 1951 | 1931 | 1951 |
| Occupational class of fathers | | | | |
| Professional | 5% | 17% | 24% | 32% |
| Business-managerial | 27 | 21 | 27 | 34 |
| Farmer | 2 | – | 19 | 7 |
| Other | 37 | 41 | 11 | 16 |
| Unknown | 29 | 22 | 19 | 11 |
| Total percent | 100% | 101% | 100% | 100% |
| Ethnic status | | | | |
| "Old Stock" | 9% | 6% | 89% | 57% |
| Irish | 39 | 33 | 5 | 11 |
| Jews | 43 | 38 | – | 2 |
| Italians | 4 | 20 | 3 | 9 |
| Others | – | 1 | – | 14 |
| Unknown | 5 | 1 | 3 | 7 |
| Total percent | 100% | 99% | 100% | 100% |
| Types of law schools attended | | | | |
| High entrance, full-time | 5% | 14% | 30% | 20% |
| Low entrance, full-time | 2 | – | 43 | 57 |
| Low entrance, part-time | 88 | 86 | 11 | 16 |
| Short course and non-attendance* | 5 | – | 16 | 7 |
| Total percent | 100% | 100% | 100% | 100% |
| Total number | 56 | 69 | 37 | 44 |

* Non-attendance refers to a situation where the lawyer did not go to school but passed his bar examination through means of correspondence courses and/or guidance of established lawyers.

New York, a candidate's ethnic qualities could be counted as an asset, likely to generate appeal to the immigrant-based electorate. A complementary asset has been the profession of law. Through hard experience, many ambitious New York City politicians have found this occupation to be a useful and ofttimes necessary instrument of political advancement. For those who succeeded in acquiring the combination of law and politics, the long-run goal has tended to be the judgeship.[14] Once established, this pattern of socio-political mobility has not only persisted, but it has become more pronounced, even as ethnic wealth has accumulated and occupational discrimination has diminished.

---

14. Among the 1931 and 1951 legislative personnel, there is no evidence that Negroes had as yet developed this technique of advancement.

# 8

# LEGISLATIVE LEADERS

As compared to other similar institutions, the New York legislature has had more than its share of outstanding achievers. Though some, such as Theodore Roosevelt and Franklin D. Roosevelt, never managed to distinguish themselves in its chambers,[1] there were others who were successful in using the institution as a proving ground for higher leadership. In the twentieth century this includes Governor Alfred E. Smith, Democratic candidate for President in 1928, and such notables as James W. Wadsworth, Jr., Irving M. Ives, and Robert F. Wagner, Sr., all respected members of the United States Senate.

Lawmakers take pride in pointing to such heroes of the recent past; and justifiably so, for the institutions and communities they serve can generally be no better than the leadership provided. Where responsible leadership does not come forth, the community suffers. With this in mind, we now attempt to assess New York legislative leaders. Who are they? Where do they come from? Where do they go? In the previous chapter it was discerned that legislators no longer move into major statewide office. How can this be explained with reference to ranking personnel? Can it be said that stewardship in the lawmaking body is no longer an adequate apprenticeship for greater responsibility in the polity?

---

1. Interestingly, both men were of aristocratic backgrounds and both took a rather dim view of their legislative surroundings.

## ELECTIVE PARTY OFFICERS

The locus of power in most American legislatures is ordinarily found in its party and committee leadership. In some such bodies, like the United States Congress, competition between the standing-committee chairmen and the elected party leaders (e.g., Speaker, majority leaders) is so nearly balanced that there results some considerable diffusion of power. In the New York legislature, however, the party leadership overawes all and is probably more controlling than is the case for most such agencies. To illustrate, a former Speaker of the Assembly, a Republican observes:

> The Legislature is more highly organized than any other in the world—bar none. Never once in the fifteen years I've been there have we failed to get a Republican majority for a "must" piece of legislation. We Republicans have a tradition of discipline. Any new member is immediately schooled in that tradition of Republican control.[2]

The reasons for this claim are clear enough. It is the Speaker, as party leader, who appoints members to committees and chairmanships, dispenses a personal payroll of more than two million dollars a year and can decide, as chairman of the Rules Committee, which bills are to be allowed out of committee for floor consideration. Any lawmaker who resists the Speaker's directives must prepare himself for some disquieting consequences.

But successful leadership is contingent on factors other than formal techniques of control. Since legislative leaders usually cannot directly influence members' chances for renomination and reelection, they must also depend on persuasion and bargaining with their following. Those who can do such things best vary with time and circum-

2. Joseph Carlino in the New York *Post*, February 2, 1960.

stance. New conditions require new skills, especially as institutional membership changes. That which interests us, specifically, is to discern the requisite traits of party leaders over time. What types of persons best manage to apply themselves to the tasks of persuading and accommodating? What are their career perspectives? What changes have taken place, and why? Where party control is as strong as it is in the New York legislature, some answers here, it is believed, will convey important understanding into the legislative process.

## The evolving pattern of legislative leadership

In scrutinizing the key leadership positions—i.e., Speaker and Majority Leader of the Assembly and President Pro Tem of the Senate—from the 1920s to the late 1960s (see Table 36), it is clear that the Republican party has long been dominant. Until 1964 when reapportionment was effected, the Democrats were relegated primarily to the minority leadership roles—i.e., Assembly and Senate Minority Leaders. Under such circumstances it was the rural-oriented Patrons who were initially in control. Stressing laissez-faire and the traditional shibboleths of small-town life, e.g., "small government is best," they were known as the Old Guard. This is how Warren Moscow describes them:

> In up-state New York many a [political leader] was also president of the local bank, owner of the local power company, which grew up from the little generator at the site of the old mill dam and was absorbed later in a state-wide combine, with himself as a big stockholder. He was generally the chief local representative of the established economic order, and as such was also Republican. . . .[3]

Both H. Edmund Machold and Joseph A. McGinnies, who, together, held the Assembly Speakership from 1921

3. *Politics in the Empire State,* p. 71.

to 1934, come fairly close to this stereotype. It was the 1929 stock-market crash and the ensuing depression that signaled the demise of such leadership. But an additional factor, certainly, was that growing urbanization in the state gave call to a new kind of leadership.

In 1935, Oswald Heck of Schenectady was elected Speaker over the opposition of the old rural bloc; and thereafter, the upstate city interests in alliance with suburban districts were able to effect more liberal programs. Upon Heck's death in 1959, the "new men" of suburbia moved into the ascendancy.[4] Joseph Carlino of Long Island assumed the top command post in the Assembly and held on for the next five years. And in 1966, Perry B. Duryea, also of Long Island, became the Republican Minority Leader after having upset the short reign of an upstater. (Not included in our statistics is that Duryea became Speaker in 1969.) It wasn't until the 1950s that a new pattern could be noted in the Senate. From 1954 to 1964, the President Pro Tem (or Majority Leader) of that chamber was Walter Mahoney who represented the second largest city in the state, i.e., Buffalo. And after his electoral defeat, Earl W. Brydges of Niagara Falls (a city of about 90,000 population) took charge.

More recently, reapportionment has tended to put Democratic types in full control of the Assembly. Such persons are from New York City, are primarily of Irish or Jewish background, and are usually employed as lawyers. But the Senate, which remains as a Republican enclave, still tends to evade them.

Overall, it appears that as leader-based constituencies have become more urbanized, the legislative standard-bearers no longer manifest the qualities of the gentlemanly Patron. Rather, it is the career politician who has come of age. As previously described, he is a person who

---

4. Table 36 distinguishes suburban legislative leaders with an asterisk (*) in the 2,500+ category.

Table 36. Characteristics of Legislative Leaders from 1920 to 1967

| Characteristics | 1920–1929 | | 1930–1939 | | 1940–1949 | | 1950–1959 | | 1960–1967 | | Total | |
|---|---|---|---|---|---|---|---|---|---|---|---|---|
| | Dem. | Rep. | Dem. | Rep. | Dem. | Rep. | Dem. | Rep. | Dem. | Rep. | Dem. | Rep. |
| **Leadership position** | | | | | | | | | | | | |
| Ass. Speaker | — | 3 | 1 | 2 | — | 1 | — | 1 | — | 1 | 2 | 6 |
| Sen. Pres. Pro Tem | 1 | 3 | 1 | 3 | — | 2 | — | 1 | — | 1 | 3 | 10 |
| Ass. Maj. Leader | — | 2 | 1 | — | — | 1 | — | 1 | — | 1 | 2 | 5 |
| Sen. Min. Leader | 1 | — | — | — | — | — | 1 | — | 1 | — | 3 | — |
| Ass. Min. Leader | 2 | — | — | — | 1 | — | 1 | — | — | — | 3 | 1 |
| Total | 4 | 8 | 3 | 5 | 1 | 3 | 2 | 2 | 3 | 3 | 13 | 22 |
| **Type of district** | | | | | | | | | | | | |
| New York City | 4 | — | 3 | — | 1 | — | 2 | — | 3 | — | 13 | — |
| 100,000+ | — | 2 | — | 1 | — | 1 | — | — | — | — | — | 5 |
| 25,000+ | — | — | — | 1 | — | — | — | 1 | — | 1 | — | 3 |
| 2,500+ | — | 3 | — | — | — | 1 | — | 1* | — | 1* | — | 6 |
| –2,500 | — | 3 | — | 3 | — | 2 | — | — | — | 2 | — | 8 |
| Total | 4 | 8 | 3 | 5 | 1 | 3 | 2 | 2 | 3 | 3 | 13 | 22 |
| **Ethnicity** | | | | | | | | | | | | |
| "Old Stock" | — | 6 | — | 4 | — | 2 | — | 2 | — | 2 | — | 16 |
| Irish | 3 | — | 2 | — | — | 1 | 2 | — | 1 | — | 8 | 1 |
| Jewish | 1 | 1 | 1 | 1 | 1 | — | — | 2 | 1 | — | 4 | 2 |
| Italian | — | — | — | 1 | — | — | — | 1 | 1 | — | — | 1 |
| German | — | 1 | — | — | — | — | — | — | — | 1 | 1 | 2 |
| Total | 4 | 8 | 3 | 5 | 1 | 3 | 2 | 2 | 3 | 3 | 13 | 22 |

156

| Occupation | | | | | | | | | | | |
|---|---|---|---|---|---|---|---|---|---|---|---|
| Business-exec. | — | 2 | 1 | 1 | — | 2 | — | — | — | 1 | 6 |
| Lawyer | 3 | 5 | 1 | 4 | 1 | 1 | 2 | 3 | 3 | 10 | 15 |
| Professional | 1 | 1 | 1 | — | — | — | — | — | — | 2 | 1 |
| Total | 4 | 8 | 3 | 5 | 1 | 3 | 2 | 3 | 3 | 13 | 22 |

Note: Legislative leaders are recorded for the highest position attained and are assigned to ten year time categories on the basis of the particular year in which they first achieved such position.

* Suburban districts.

157

Table 37. Legislative Leaders Compared with Legislative Personnel

| Characteristics | 1920–1929 N | 1920–1929 % | 1930–1939 N | 1930–1939 % | 1940–1949 N | 1940–1949 % | 1950–1959 N | 1950–1959 % | 1960–1967 N | 1960–1967 % | Total N | Total % | |
|---|---|---|---|---|---|---|---|---|---|---|---|---|---|
| | (12) | | (8) | | (4) | | (5) | | (6) | | | | |
| Under 46 yrs. when first elected to legis. | | | | | | | | | | | | | |
| Leaders | 9 | 75 | 6 | 75 | 4 | 100 | 4 | 80 | 5 | 83 | 28 | 80 | (N 35 ) |
| 1931 personnel | | | | | | | | | | | 134 | 67 | (N 201) |
| 1951 personnel | | | | | | | | | | | 133 | 65 | (N 206) |
| Prior political experience | | | | | | | | | | | | | |
| Leaders | 5 | 42 | 2 | 25 | 3 | 75 | — | — | 1 | 17 | 11 | 31 | |
| 1931 personnel | | | | | | | | | | | 83 | 41 | |
| 1951 personnel | | | | | | | | | | | 108 | 52 | |
| Extra-legislative party leadership | | | | | | | | | | | | | |
| Leaders | 3 | 25 | 2 | 25 | 1 | 25 | 4 | 80 | 4 | 66 | 14 | 40 | |
| 1931 personnel | | | | | | | | | | | 40 | 20 | |
| 1951 personnel | | | | | | | | | | | 57 | 28 | |
| Post-legislative political mobility | | | | | | | | | | | | | |
| Leaders | 6 | 50 | 3 | 38 | 2 | 50 | 1 | 20 | 1 | 17* | 13 | 37 | |
| 1931 personnel | | | | | | | | | | | 86 | 43 | |
| 1951 personnel | | | | | | | | | | | 78 | 38† | |

*Five out of six leaders were still in the legislature at the time of writing, 1967.
†Eight percent of the 1951 personnel were still in the legislature at the time of writing, 1967.

158

manifests a decided commitment to politics in terms of personal stakes and pursues a political career with great persistence. First, Table 37 shows that the party leaders are generally elected to the legislature at a much earlier age than is the average legislator, a sign of early political involvement. Second, a smaller proportion of them appear to dally in the lower echelons of government but set their sights directly toward the legislature where there is greater initial prestige. Third, a much higher percentage of them show experience in managing the affairs of extra-legislative party organizations, e.g., county chairmen, district leaders.

Our expectations falter, however, in the matter of post-legislative advancement. The data indicate that since the 1930s, the rate of political mobility for leaders has gradually decreased and has fallen below that which is found for lawmakers generally. Nor is it the case that many move off to important statewide office when they do advance.[5] Undoubtedly one reason for this is that as ranking members of the legislature, they are, next to the Governor, the most powerful men in the state. It is understandable, therefore, that they should be reluctant to take their leave. An additional consideration is that as the

5. The following reveals post-legislative political mobility according to the highest position achieved by mobile legislative leaders.

| Type of position | No. of mobiles | Period of leadership | Party |
|---|---|---|---|
| Federal: Congress | 1 | 1920–1929 | Republican |
|     Judiciary | 2 | 1920–1929 | 2 Republicans |
|     Senate | 1 | 1930–1939 | Republican |
| State: Judiciary | 2 | 1920–1929, 1950–1959 | 1 Dem., 1 Repub. |
|     Lt. Governor | 1 | 1930–1939 | Republican |
|     Dept. or Cmn. head | 3 | 1940–1949, 1960–1967 | 3 Republicans |
| City: Mayor (N.Y.C.) | 1 | 1920–1929 | Democrat |
|     Court Clerk | 1 | 1930–1939 | Democrat |
| Local: County Clerk | 1 | 1920–1929 | Republican |

visible commanders and spokesmen of the two major
parties, they, more than anyone else in the legislature,
symbolize the continuing rift which exists between upstate
Republicanism and downstate Democracy; this serves as
a weighty impediment should they attempt to garner
broad electoral support.[6] But no matter what the explanation, we have discerned a situation worthy of serious concern. Leadership skills developed in the lawmaking body
are not readily used elsewhere in politics; and this is more
true today than ever before.

## COMMITTEE CHAIRMEN

Because of the very substantial number of legislative
proposals introduced each year and because of their growing complexity, the legislature is compelled to depend
increasingly on its committees. It is here where the real
work of preparing, considering and modifying measures
goes on. In New York, this situation, as measured by the
number of bills introduced each session, is more pronounced than in any other state in the union.[7] Furthermore, the inability of the lawmaking body to give adequate consideration to its many bills usually necessitates
near unequivocal acceptance of committee recommendations. It has been estimated that in the New York legislature, close to forty percent of all bills die in committees
while more than ninety percent of all committee recommendations are accepted by both houses.[8] It can be seen
that under such conditions the "little legislatures," as they
are often called, assume significant power. This is espe-

---

6. This will be made more vivid when we later treat the careers of
Joe R. Hanley from upstate New York and Anthony J. Travia from
New York City.

7 See *The Book of the States, 1966–67* (Chicago: Council of State Governments, 1966) pp. 62–63.

8. Lynton K. Caldwell, *The Government and Administration of New
York* (New York: Thomas Y. Crowell Co., 1954), p. 69.

cially true of the chairmen, each one of whom is in charge
of his own unit with extensive authority of command.[9]

Lawmakers who can qualify pursue chairmanships with
considerable alacrity. The rewards of such posts are
ofttimes greater than one would ordinarily suspect. This
includes staff, which is a source of patronage, and extra
compensation which can presently range as high as
$18,000 in selected instances. Note the following inquiry
from an aspiring chairman to one who is about to depart:

> Some times there is such an overwhelming demand for
> some certain person that the Speaker has to overlook rank
> and take some other person.
> I would like to know your honest opinion, do I stand
> any chance? If not I do not want to ask my friends to inter-
> cede for me and go to a lot of trouble that will amount to
> nothing. If I do stand a chance I can have my organization
> ask for the appointment along with some others.
> By the way it is the Banks Comm. I am speaking of and
> I surely need close contact with them after this terrible
> slump. I found two dollars in an old suit the other day and
> it made me feel like a million dollars.[10]

*A lesson in cultural lag*

As previously discerned, until 1964, it was the small
towns and rural areas which were overrepresented in the
legislature. Under such circumstances, the Patrons of a
bygone era could hold on as committee chairmen, fending
off "unsound" ideas which appeared to threaten traditional society. The data in Table 38 on the State Assembly offer some indication of their qualities: more of them

9. Chairmen are appointed and can be removed by the party leaders,
e.g., Speaker, President Pro Tem. Thus they do not have the same degree of independence as in legislatures where seniority is the prime pre-
requisite.
10. The letter is dated November 16, 1929. From the Bert Lord Papers,
Collection of Regional History and University Archives, Cornell University.

Table 38. Comparison of Committee Chairmen, Republicans and All Legislators in the Assembly by Selected Characteristics, 1931 and 1951.

| Characteristics | Ass. Chmn. | | Ass. Repubs. | | Assemblymen | |
|---|---|---|---|---|---|---|
| | 1931 | 1951 | 1931 | 1951 | 1931 | 1951 |
| | (N 33) | (N 36) | (N 80) | (N 87) | (N 150) | (N 150) |
| Type of district | | | | | | |
| New York City | –% | 11% | 3% | 11% | 41% | 45% |
| 100,000+ | 18 | 8 | 17 | 13 | 13 | 10 |
| 25,000+ | 9 | 11 | 17 | 14 | 10 | 9 |
| 2,500+ | 21 | 25 | 17 | 23 | 10 | 13 |
| –2,500 | 52 | 45 | 45 | 39 | 26 | 23 |
| Occupational class | | | | | | |
| Professionals | 33% | 36% | 39% | 47% | 55% | 59% |
| Proprietors & officials | 15 | 28 | 20 | 21 | 13 | 14 |
| Small businessmen, semi-professional & technical | 18 | 25 | 16 | 18 | 12 | 15 |
| Farmers | 30 | 11 | 21 | 9 | 12 | 5 |
| Ethnics* | 3% | 8% | 4% | 16% | 39% | 48% |
| Non-Protestants | 6% | 17% | 6% | 29% | 43% | 52% |
| Age: Under 46 years | 30% | 20% | 36% | 27% | 56% | 47% |
| Age when first elected to legis.: Under 46 years | 48% | 55% | 51% | 56% | 68% | 66% |
| Party leadership (extra-legislative) | 36% | 25% | 22% | 25% | 21% | 27% |
| Prior political experience | 67% | 53% | 66% | 61% | 40% | 52% |
| Post-legislative mobility | 36% | 30%† | 43% | 31%† | 48% | 39%† |

*Only the numerically most important ethnic groups are treated here. These are the Italians, Irish, Jews and Negroes.

†No chairmen, two percent of all Assembly Republicans and seven percent of all Assemblymen were still in the legislature at the time of writing (1967).

are elderly, rural and native Protestant than are Republicans generally, not to speak of all Assemblymen.[11]

There is every indication that change in the social make-up of such ranking policy-makers would have been very slow in coming if not for the Supreme Court case *WMCA v. Lomenzo*. Prior to 1964, upstate rural types were giving way gradually; but even in 1961, big-city representatives were near powerless (see Table 39). Contrast this with the data for 1965, after reapportionment was effected; the change is radical. As the Democrats came to power, so too did the New York City ethnics. Farmers and native Protestants virtually disappeared.

Of additional interest here is that as a result of such transformation, new forms of legislation were for the first time brought forth from the committees. Within a few short years, provisions for the sale of alcoholic beverages and restrictions of the state's 179-year-old divorce law were liberalized. A comprehensive revision of anti-discrimination laws and a new program to combat narcotics addiction are other examples. Even the sensitive topic of legalized abortion has been permitted serious consideration though no legal revisions have as yet been made. All these matters reflect the essentially urban character of the new leadership.

## CAREER STRATEGY: TWO CASES

Every career-oriented individual who is committed to political advancement must give careful consideration to the various opportunities available to him. In devising strategy he must be sure to weigh not only his own special

11. The information which follows is based upon the characteristics of Assembly chairmen only. The Senate is not considered because of the fact that almost all members of the majority party in this chamber are elevated to chairmanships. Where nearly all Republicans become chairmen, which was the case in 1931 and 1951, generalization about chairmen is, in effect, generalization about Senate Republicans.

Table 39. Characteristics of Assembly Committee Chairmen for 1931, 1951, 1961, and 1965.

| Characteristics | 1931 | 1951 | 1961 | 1965 |
|---|---|---|---|---|
| Type of district | | | | |
| New York City | —% | 11% | 14% | 80% |
| 100,000+ | 18 | 8 | 6 | 14 |
| 25,000+ | 9 | 11 | 8 | 6 |
| 2,500+ | 21 | 25 | 28 | — |
| —2,500 | 52 | 45 | 44 | — |
| Total | 100% | 100% | 100% | 100% |
| Occupation | | | | |
| Professional | 33% | 36% | 54% | 69% |
| Business-exec.* | 24% | 50% | 37% | 11% |
| Farmer | 30% | 11% | 11% | —% |
| Ethnics | 3% | 8% | 19% | 89% |
| Non-Protestant | 6% | 17% | 33% | 97% |
| Total number | 33 | 36 | 36 | 36 |

*This includes small businessmen.

abilities and traits but also various conditions in the political system which might facilitate or obstruct his aspirations.

Among other things, he must ask: What are the "rules," both formal and informal, which he must heed? To whom must he look for support and whom and what must he avoid lest he be impeded?

To the extent that the politics of a society is well structured, the personal risks involved can be held to a minimum; for the aspirant is then better able to discern the various stages of promotion and assess the kind of resources and skills required. The more open the politics, the less predictable it becomes and the greater the risks of seeking advancement. In New York, the system is well structured on the lower levels of the career ladder but becomes increasingly diffuse on the higher levels. As was

previously observed, New York City Democrats and upstate Republicans who serve in the state legislature need
have little fear of inter-party competition during elections; nor are party primaries of much worry in the average district. So long as the candidate fulfills his obligations
of party regularity and loyalty, and so long as he shows
"dedication" to major constituency interests, he can look
to the future with a reasonable degree of confidence. However, it is when the aspirant begins to think in terms of
statewide office that his troubles mount. To illustrate,
compare the career histories of two men who *almost* made
it to the Governorship.

## The case of a small-town contender

It was during the Republican state nominating convention of 1934 that Joe R. Hanley projected himself as a
political contender worthy of serious consideration.
Elected permanent chairman of that body, Hanley's acceptance address brought delegates to their feet in what
observers called the most spontaneous outburst that had
occured in a state convention in years. According to the
New York *Herald-Tribune*:

> By the time he had finished his address, the convention
> was so excited that it became apparent immediately that he
> was timber worthy of a place on the ticket. In fact, F. Tru-
> bee Davison, chairman of the Republican Legislative Com-
> paign Committee . . . came over to the press table and
> announced that he would like to have Mr. Hanley for
> United States Senator.[12]

Unfortunately, the time was not ripe for such auspicious
plans, for the party potentates had already settled upon
the candidates. But hereafter, Hanley's dream of high office took on a special vividness. The big question for him

12. September 29, 1934.

was how long would it be before the dream became reality.

Prior to this development, Joe R. Hanley's career had been long and varied. Born in Davenport, Iowa, in 1876, the son of a lawyer, he graduated twenty-three years later from Iowa State University with a Bachelor of Laws degree. He was undecided, however, whether to be a lawyer or a clergyman. While practicing law as a member of his father's firm, he continued his education at Iowa Wesleyan College. In 1902, upon receiving a Doctor of Divinity degree, he entered the ministry in the Iowa Conference of the Methodist Episcopal Church. After nine years in this occupation, he left to travel as an evangelist in the United States and Canada. No doubt it was during this time that he developed his skill as a speaker. It was also part of his experience during these early years to have served his country in the Spanish-American War and later as a chaplain in the First World War.

In May, 1923, Mr. Hanley moved wtih his family to New York where he accepted the pastorate at the Brick Presbyterian Church in the village of Perry. It was in this small, sleepy community (population 4,600) that he was to combine his many talents in the pursuit of the profession of politics. At the beginning, success was pretty well assured. As a Mason, Rotarian, decorated veteran of two wars, minister, lawyer and Republican, he manifested many of the trappings admired and respected in small-town America. And if there were still some doubts as to his abilities, his evangelical style of oratory was the clincher—at least for the majority of home folks.

Having served in the Assembly for five years, he was elected to the State Senate in 1931. Here he continued to work as a loyal Republican, wandering neither too far to the left nor to the right of the party line. Speechmaking became his finest asset, preaching the tried and true ideas of a party which still could not perceive or understand the total impact of the opposition New Deal. For example: "We will learn some day that there is only one real way to reduce taxes. Cease spending so much money." "We Republicans stand for more business in state government and less government in business."[13]

When the time came for the Republicans to select a new leader in the upper house, the previous one having died, Hanley's name was one of those prominently mentioned. Considered only as an outside possibility at first, the Republican caucus took note of the fact that his record had not left him "tagged" as either a conservative or a radical liberal; and on the sixth ballot he was chosen as the compromise candidate most acceptable to the opposing factions. As the new leader of the majority party, his election to the post of Senate President Pro Tem was simply a matter of form—the eventful day was February 27, 1939. In reporting the election, the press explained it as a victory for the rural bloc of Republicans in their continuing confrontation with urban party leaders.

Opportunity knocked again when the incumbent Lieutenant Governor died in July, 1943, and Mr. Hanley, as Senate leader, became acting Lieutenant Governor. In a special election in the fall of 1943, he was elected to the office; and in 1946, with the re-election of Republican Governor Thomas E. Dewey, Hanley won a full term.

Henceforth and unavoidably, Hanley's career would be closely connected with the political plans of Governor Dewey. The older of the two, Hanley could not hope for the state's highest office until Dewey moved on. To make matters even more complicated, Dewey was a leading Republican contender for the presidential office as has been the case for almost every New York Governor in the twentieth century. If Dewey felt strong disappointment in twice suffering defeat in presidential elections, undoubtedly Hanley did too; especially in 1948 when, as Lieutenant

13. The Perry *Herald*, October 3, 1934.

Governor, the latter would have succeded directly to the Governorship.

In June of 1950, it suddenly appeared as if Hanley's long-awaited chance had come at last. Dewey announced he would not seek a third term to the gubernatorial office. Barely forty-eight hours after the announcement, Hanley, as heir apparent, issued a typewritten statement as follows:

> As Mr. Dewey has announced he will not run this fall, I will be a candidate, subject to the will of the delegates to the convention. If nominated, I will conduct an intensive and aggressive campaign, and if elected, I will carry on the same kind of progressive, constructive, liberal administration that has been in effect the past eight years, and of which I have been a part.[14]

But no sooner was the candidacy proclaimed than events began to take a peculiar turn. Dewey himself was apparently uncertain about his being replaced by a man who was seventy-four years old. There were newspaper reports of mounting pressure within the party urging the Governor to reconsider his decision. Only a few days before the Republican nominating convention, Hanley issued another statement revealing the text of a letter sent to Dewey.

> My Dear Governor:
>
> On June 17, 1950, when you stated to me you would not be a candidate at the fall election and offered to support me for Governor, I gladly announced my candidacy for office.
>
> May I respectfully suggest that since then we have become embroiled in a conflict that threatens to become worldwide (the Korean War). Because of the great danger to the nation and our State and because you are more experienced in handling the affairs of the State in time of crisis than any other citizen, I feel impelled to release you from your pledge of support and to urge that you consent to seek

14. The *New York Times*, June 20, 1950.

re-election this fall with the assurance that I will support you in every way I possibly can.[15]

At about the same time, Hanley indicated a willingness to run for United States Senator instead; and he subsequently accepted the nomination when it was offered.

Shortly after, on the eve of the convention, another letter was written by Hanley—a secret one. The recipient was W. Kingsland Macy, Suffolk County Republican Chairman and a former Republican State Chairman. Hanley wrote:

> Today I had a conference with the Governor in which certain unalterable and unquestionably definite propositions were made to me, if I will consent to take the nomination to the United States Senate, I am definitedly assured of being able to clean up my financial obligations within ninety days, so that I would be clear for the first time in twenty years of my life. I am assured of an adequate living compensation if elected, in a perfectly legal and unquestionable way. Also I have an iron-clad, unbreakable arrangement whereby I will be given a job with the state which I would like and enjoy (I have been told what it is) at sufficient compensation to make my net income more than I now have. This removes all gamble from the picture and will enable me to face the future with confidence that, even if I lost my eyesight, I would still have a comfortable living and be able to do the duties devolving upon me.[16]

Further along in the letter, Hanley assures Macy "that within a short time you will receive from me every cent that I owe you, and at least you will not lose that part of the investment." He then describes himself as "humiliated, disappointed and heart sick."

In acting as he did, two things seemed to have been of

---

15. The *New York Times*, September 3, 1950.
16. The letter was dated September 5, 1950, and was publicly revealed in the *New York Times* and the press generally on October 17, 1950.

immediate concern to Hanley: his failing eyesight, possibly leading to total blindness, and the obligation to pay off long-standing family debts. Thus his desperately felt need for material security and for assurance as to his future well-being. But the letter also highlights bitter factionalism within the Republican party. The "investment" which Hanley refers to was money he owed to Mr. Macy as well as to one Frank E. Gannett, noted newspaper publisher; it was money which they had advanced for the pre-convention campaign. Throughout the pre-convention maneuvering, they were the leaders of a group which backed Hanley with the belief that his candidacy for Governor would finally remove Dewey from his long-time role of leadership in New York politics. Once Dewey changed his mind and decided to run after all, Hanley became the key figure: only he could free Dewey from his pledge of abstention. Unless Hanley so decided, Dewey would have been morally obligated to refuse the convention nomination. Reportedly faced with the prospect of losing substantial support at the convention, Hanley agreed not to run. His nomination to the office of United States Senator was the consolation prize.

As for the letter itself, it turned out to be a poorly kept secret. Someone, allegedly Mr. Macy, photographed the letter for distribution to the "right" persons. The likely motive: to show that the Dewey "draft" was not genuine, but one that could have occurred only with the Govenor himself applying pressure on Hanley. To complicate the matter further, at least one copy of the letter got into the hands of high-ranking Democrats. In light of this, there seemed to be no way out for Hanley but to publicly reveal the letter to the press and explain it as best he could.

What was the reaction of others who were involved? Mr. Gannett admitted the truth to the loan while Macy would offer no comment. Governor Dewey said that he was "delighted" that the Lieutenant Governor had "met the smear attack head-on." As for offering Hanley a state job, the Governor explained: "Nearly two years ago we talked of that possibility. I told him that the state could ill afford to lose his services. Any time he is prepared to accept an appointment, I consider it a great honor."[17]

If the letter had any adverse effects, it was with respect to Mr. Hanley and not Mr. Dewey. The latter was re-elected over his Democratic opponent by 573,000 votes. The former lost to his opponent by 261,000 votes. With respect to Dewey's pledge of a job, Mr. Hanley was appointed as special counsel to the State Division of Veterans Affairs about a month after the elections. The position paid $16,000 a year plus $4,000 for expenses. In addition, as special counsel, Hanley served on a contract basis rather than as a regular state employee; in this way he was able to draw his pension amounting to about $4,200. He retained the office until it was abolished in 1955 by a new Democratic Governor, Averell Harriman.

## The case of a big-city aspirant

The son of a barber, Assemblyman Anthony John Travia represented the district in Brooklyn where he first moved to at the age of fifteen. From the very beginning, Mr. Travia manifested a willingness to work hard in order to make his way in the world, washing dishes in a cafeteria and serving subpoenas while attending evening law school. It was during this youthful period that he got his first taste of politics, campaigning on the back of a truck for Alfred E. Smith, Democratic candidate for President. "The bug bit me and I stayed bitten," he later recalled. "I found out I loved politics."

Elected to the New York Assembly in 1943 at the age of thirty-one, it was another twenty-two years before Travia could reach the topmost legislative office, i.e., Speaker. There were many disappointments and barriers to be

17. The *New York Times,* October 17, 1950.

overcome along the way. After serving his first two terms in the legislature, he was defeated in the Dewey gubernatorial victory of 1946. He managed to return two years later, however. In 1951, Mr. Travia got in trouble with the Liberal party (which usually endorses Democrats) when he sponsored a bill tightening the law on circulation of party nomination petitions. The measure, passed into law, required that persons performing the job be party members and residents of the district in which they were working. As such, it was criticized as a threat to independent candidacies. The following year, Travia sponsored three bills limiting political activity by labor unions; these did not pass. But his performance here cost him the Liberal party nomination in 1952. (Though he was nominated by the Democrats since the New York election law permits multiple party nominations.)

Hereafter, Travia was to be more careful and through a combination of skill and luck he moved steadily ahead. In 1956, he became Democratic party leader of the twenty-second Assembly District, thus consolidating his control over his constituency. Three years later, due in part to a fortuitous set of circumstances, he was elected Minority Leader of the New York Assembly. This came about through the need of the party to mitigate factionalism and maintain a balance of interests. Accordingly, one of the unwritten rules is that the Democratic legislative leadership be divided between Manhattan and Brooklyn and between a Catholic and a Jew. Since the Minority Leader in the Senate was a Manhattan Jew, Travia met the eligibility requirements as a Brooklyn Catholic. In addition, he had seniority over other contenders and, to his credit, he had acquired the reputation of being a "go-getter." While there were those who spoke of certain personal defects—e.g., poor oratorical style, heavy-handed negotiator— such matters were considered to be of secondary importance.

In 1964, presidential politics gave the New York Democrats an unexpected assist. For the first time in thirty years they were able to achieve majority control of the legislature and, along with it, all the important leadership positions. But the initial glee over their victory quickly disappeared—unaccustomed to their new-found authority, the Democrats became victim to factionalism. During the first thirty-five days of the 1965 legislative session, a deadlock occurred over who would fill the posts of State Majority Leader and Assembly Speaker. With the Republicans backing their own candidates, neither of the two competing Democratic groups could command the required majority in either chamber.

It was a rare and unexpected ploy that finally settled the contest. Governor Rockefeller directed the Republicans to vote for Travia in the Assembly and Zaretski in the Senate. In return, it was rumored, the two new leaders would deliver Democratic votes to support some aspects of the Governor's program. (At a later date, Rockefeller did get such assistance in the form of a new sales tax he had requested.) In the first blush of victory, Travia could only express the hope that all would be forgotten with no recriminations. But the bitterness of the losing side hung heavy in the air as they spoke of a "sellout."

As Speaker, Travia's luck held. When the Democrats controlled both houses of the legislature in 1965, he had to share the limelight with Joseph Zaretski, Majority Leader of the Senate. But in 1966, a split legislature was returned by the voters, putting the Republicans in control of the upper house. With Zaretski reduced to Minority Leader again, the Speaker's standing assumed greater significance. Furthermore, with the New York City mayoralty going to Republican-Liberal John Lindsay in 1965 (usually a Democratic office), only one other Democrat remained who held a position of power in the state—Senator Robert F. Kennedy.

In state politics, then, Travia had reached the top. It was he whom Governor Rockefeller had to deal with if the public machinery was to move effectively. As the Speaker explained: "The Governor's a great guy; we get along. He's a great con artist. He gets his pound of flesh and, believe me, I get mine. After all, I could kill any of his bills."[18]

It would be incorrect to attribute Mr. Travia's success to good fortune alone; for in using his authority he has shown considerable political astuteness. After the hard-fought battle in which he was elected Speaker, he took care to appoint opposing Democratic legislators to important chairmanships; and good committee assignments were given to Reform Democrats, a group of party insurgents. In addition, he managed to enhance his liberal image by pushing through the lawmaking body a $1.50 minimum wage as well as one of the most far-reaching public medical-care programs in the country. Consequently, in the succeeding three party elections (1966, 1967 and 1968) Travia won unanimous support for the Speakership.

What next? Intrigued with the rough and tumble of political life, Travia had kept one eye on the Govenor's seat. Indeed, for a time there was a glimmer of hope that his presidency of the New York State Constitutional Convention in 1967 would serve as a stepping-stone in this direction. On adjournment of the Convention, several delegates put on "Travia for Governor" buttons, remnants of a half-hearted effort for nomination during the previous year. But when the proposed constitution was turned down by the voters by a wide margin, the possibilities for such advancement quickly faded.

Another career alternative for Travia had been a judge-ship. For years, since he became leader of the Democrats,

18. Richard Reeves, "The Other Half of the State Government," The *New York Times Magazine*, April, 1967, p. 25.

the rumor mills produced reports of his eventual move-ment to the quietude of judicial office. Certainly, as we've seen, the prestige of the office, if not the income, is a weighty inducement for any man. Yet, this too presented problems. Simmering beneath the surface was the old fac-tional feud which was manifest in the 1965 battle over the Speaker's position. It was feared that Mr. Travia's de-parture from the legislature might trigger another party fight, something to be avoided at all costs.

On April 25, 1968, Mr. Travia's fate was decided. Presi-dent Lyndon B. Johnson nominated him to the United States District Court for the Eastern District of New York. Upon receiving the news, Travia said he was "very honored and privileged. . . . It's like a Horatio Alger story for me."[19] As for the expected Speakership fight, a suc-cessor was selected by the Democratic legislative caucus the following January with barely anything more than a whimper. Of some relevance to this is that the Democrats had lost the Assembly in the November elections and the only thing at stake was the post of Assembly Minority Leader.

*Summation and conclusions*

Joseph A. Schlesinger contends that ambition, not principles or ideology, is the very essence of politics.[20] In this light, a politician's behavior can best be under-stood as a reflection of his office goals. "Or, to put it an-other way, the politician as office seeker engages in political acts and makes decisions appropriate to gaining office. His problem consists, first, in defining his office goal or goals and, secondly, in relating his current activity to them."[21]

Such a conceptualization can be related to New York's legislative leaders, many of whom, having risen so far, evi-denced ambition toward still higher office. In the cases

19. The *New York Times*, April 26, 1968.
20. *Ambition and Politics*, pp. 1–3.
21. *Ibid.*, p. 6.

studied, two very different persons, from very different types of social milieu, were directing themselves toward the same high office—the Governorship. For each, the strategy of advancement had to be specially devised to meet the particular conditions at hand.

To get his career under way, Mr. Hanley had to adopt those manners and traits which were most likely to appeal to his provincial constituents. Most important is that he had already manifested many of the necessary characteristics quite naturally, as a reflection of his own acculturation. Hanley's speeches, tempered by many years of experience as an evangelical preacher, drew upon the values of agrarian, small-town life—e.g., heavy emphasis on man's go-it-alone sense of individualism. Mr. Travia, on the other hand, projects a very different image. Gravel-voiced, dark-featured and always well clothed, he has appeared to many, particularly the upstater, as the epitome of the hard-driving, urban politico. Indeed, his manners as well as his phrasing seem to reflect his many years of involvement in club-house politics; wherever feasible, the accent is placed on such maxims as loyalty, fraternity and hierarchy.

As each one of our subjects made his way up the career ladder, some of his basic qualities had to be modified to fit changing circumstances. To quote from Schlesinger, the "ambitious politician must act in terms of the electorate of the office which he hopes to win tomorrow."[22] Thus Hanley and Travia had to begin thinking in terms of a statewide constituency. The big test for the former was when he served as Lieutenant Governor; and for the latter it was when he served as President of the New York State Constitutional Convention. Of significance is the fact that no one of them could quite overcome his early conditioning where the fundamental concern was to pro-

---

22. *Ibid.*

ject a strong appeal to a particular constituency or section within the state. Hanley ultimately became tabbed as the rural old-timer unlikely to draw sufficient electoral support from the large cities. Travia came to be seen as someone who is too much the New York City politician, unable to sustain upstate confidence. Ironically, the very qualities which initially supported their political careers on the local level subsequently served to detract from their advancement opportunities in the larger sphere of statewide politics.

Another fact of political life is that any aspirant needs others—associates, groups, the press, party leaders—for support in achieving his office goals. The more influential the allies, the greater the likelihood of success. Hanley's support came mainly from the upstate bloc of rural Republicans, which, in a state experiencing growing urbanization, was not apt to weigh heavily in his favor. His association with Governor Dewey was crucial and the latter went as far as to designate him for the gubernatorial office before reversing his decision. Resistance from Republicans who wanted a proven vote-getter (Dewey) as the state ticket-leader, as well as Dewey's own personal ambivalence, were obstacles which could not be overcome. Hanley's electoral defeat for the office of United States Senator could be attributed to all of the above-mentioned factors plus the bad press which resulted from the public revelation of his letter to Mr. Macy.

Because of the intricacies of political battle, Travia was caught in the embarrassing predicament of owing his Speakership to Governor Rockefeller, the leader of the opposition. Also playing a role in Travia's career was Senator Robert Kennedy who, by tradition of Senatorial courtesy, was able to recommend federal court nominees to the President of the United States. Though it is difficult to assess Kennedy's motivations here, there are allegations that he urged Travia for the bench so as to make the

Speaker's office available to one of his political allies. And so, the expected happened. After twenty-four years in the legislature, and realizing that the governor's office was beyond reach, the man from Brooklyn took a judgeship.

In conclusion, it can be seen that for those who aim at the highest levels of government, politics becomes a highly intricate affair where the guidelines to political behavior are fuzzy at best. And for some, like New York state legislators, the built-in obstacles have come to be near unbreachable. If the successful political leader is the type of person who can bridge the gulf which separates diverse sub-cultures, then a matter of some conjecture is whether he is any longer available through the legislature.

# 9

# CAREER BEHAVIOR AND THE
# FUNCTIONING OF THE POLITY

To perceive of legislators as merely elected office-holders who weigh and decide matters of public policy is to drastically limit the richness of insight into legislative behavior. A more refined and subtle approach is suggested by Heinz Eulau: "How they [legislators] respond and why they respond as they do are questions influenced by the whole sequence of their prior experiences, attitudes and predispositions; by their current perspectives and goals; and by their anticipation of the future. This sequence is nothing less than the political career."[1]

Thus the present study has attempted to develop a longitudinal frame of reference wherein lawmakers are assessed according to where they have been, where they are, and where they go. Of special interest has been the way in which background factors affect the typical patterns of career behavior; and then, in turn, how career behavior affects the legislature and the broader political system. As Alan Fiellin points out, certain kinds of social and political experience may substantially contribute to a person's conception of politics and the type of skills developed.[2] In addition, the career objectives of a lawmaker influences

---

1. In John C. Wahlke, *et al., The Legislative System,* p. 69.
2. Alan Fiellin, "Recruitment and Legislative Role Conceptions: A Conceptual Scheme and a Case Study," *Western Political Quarterly* 20 (June, 1967) : 274.

the way in which he defines his situation in the legislature. Is he satisfied with his present position and willing to continue there or does he see it as a steppingstone to other office? Different findings here permit us to distinguish different types of legislators in terms of political style and general performance.

Looking at all of this from a somewhat different angle, we also ask, what do career patterns tell us about the political system. As persons who are usually quite sensitive to political conditions, politicians are apt to emphasize different aspects of their careers according to different structural characteristics of the political environment. Special features of the party system—e.g., the nature and degree of party competition—would be very important here. It is expected that through an accounting of relevant variables, we can begin to assess, among other things, such intangibles as leadership and responsibility in the polity.

# Career-Patterns and "Reality Worlds"

At this point in our analysis, and by way of taking stock of much of what has preceded, career patterns are related to the individual's view of his own involvement in the legislature and politics generally—what can be called his "reality world."[3] Because the amateurs (persons who show less than ten years, overall, in public service) are so few in number, they are treated here as being incidental to other career types.

## THE PATRONS—PROTECTORS OF THE OLD ORDER

From out of the small towns and cities of upstate New York there has emerged a breed of politicians which we've

---

3. Alan Fiellin provides further elaboration of this concept, *ibid.*, pp. 276–79.

referred to as the Patrons. Primarily Republican and of old American stock, they have been concerned in protecting traditional community norms against the growing incursions of mass, urban society. Basic to their approach is the belief that fiscal retrenchment, individual effort and laissez-faire are principles which best lend sustenance to "the good life"; and where these principles are neglected or ignored, so it is that society's well-being is threatened.

Given this perspective, the Patrons look forlornly to the past when America was more agricultural than industrial and when life seemed simpler and perhaps more beautiful. As exponents of the myth of rural superiority, they fought long and hard to perpetuate a system of malapportioned legislative districts which assured the underrepresentation of urban places. When malapportionment fell by command of the Supreme Court, it signaled the beginning of the end of their influence.

Of some interest here is the fact that the very careers of the Patrons epitomize their beliefs. For a large percentage of them, the attainment of legislative office is the pinnacle of their careers, achieved after many long years of service in town, village, or county government. Such performance in local government can be considered a necessary contribution by the rural politican to the local community. It can be justified by the classic belief in grass-roots democracy, the conviction that small, home-town government represents the finest expression of popular rule and that the government closest to home is best.

Once having arrived in the legislative chambers, the Patrons manage to stay for a long while. Because they have been able to achieve positions of power and prestige in the lawmaking body, as abetted by malapportionment, relatively few of them have been inclined to depart for other office. Nor are they especially interested in the office opportunities available in the farther reaches of the political career ladder. What we have here, then, are institutionally oriented individuals who readily identify with the norms and rules of the legislature—"a home away from home." Certain issues like judicial reform and conflicts-of-interest are not likely to be as important to them as they are to the more mobile-prone careerists. Their attention, rather, is focused more directly on such public policy questions as "big government" and the state budget.

## THE CAREERISTS—"POLITICS AS A VOCATION"

The legislature, like any institution, reflects the qualities of its members; as the membership changes, so, too, does the legislature. While the Patrons strive to hold on, the amateurs—those who show a minimal amount of public office involvement—are being replaced by the careerists—those who manifest a strong personal interest in a political career. Thus, a growing professionalization of the lawmaking body has become evident.

In assessing the career politicians, it should be noted that most are Democrats from New York City. For them, a seat in the legislature is usually a beginning step, achieved at a relatively youthful age. Other than involvement in the party clubs, the greater number, by far, are recruited as political outsiders. It can be assumed that this is one reason why a large proportion of them are attorneys: legal expertise is used, in part, as a substitute for practical government experience. Furthermore, once they have arrived in the legislature, they do not stay quite as long as those from rural constituencies—their eyes are cast toward more rewarding horizons.

In terms of general perspective, the careerists tend to be preoccupied with jobs and status while relegating public issues to a lower priority of importance. Derived from families of middle to low class standing, there is indication that such persons deliberately enter politics for the purpose of making their way in the world. Indeed, most of them are of immigrant, ethnic-stock background and are thus faced with a more limited range of opportunities for climbing the class ladder.

In a sense, then, the careerist lives "off" politics; not only for the salary it affords him directly, but for the connections with business and clientele groups which become available almost automatically. As a consequence of this, conflicts-of-interest is a highly delicate issue in the legislature and, as was noted, career-minded lawmakers take a dim view of any attempt to impose restrictions on what they believe to be their personal affairs. At the same time, it was shown that a higher proportion of such persons tend to be vulnerable to the desire for "getting ahead," as evidenced by recorded acts of profligate behavior.

Of additional importance here is the use of the judgeship as a kind of ultimate reward worth waiting and fighting for. In this light, legislative service is for many a lawmaker a kind of interim period during which time he must prove his loyalty or "worthiness." To show too much independence, so as to alienate the party potentates (i.e., legislative leaders, county chairmen), could mean that the "prize" will be delayed or put permanently out of reach. Given such personal stakes, we can begin to understand the basis of legislative roadblocks to judicial reform. For there is widespread feeling among the legislators that the judiciary should not be tampered with out of fear that judgeships might then be made inaccessible; or, when this hurdle is overcome, the parties and factions which distribute such sought-after positions have found it very difficult to decide how new ones are to be apportioned.

Among the Republicans there has recently been an increase in career politicians due primarily to the rapidly expanding suburbs. Somewhat more urbane and of higher social standing than others of this type, they respond somewhat differently as well. For example, policy decisions which pertain to parks, playgrounds, schools and transportation are usually of concern to them. And they prefer to play down the more obvious forms of ethnic interplay which pervades the politics of the cities. But, as with careerists generally, they also manifest a definite preoccupation with the attainment of status through the medium of public office. Anticipating the consequences of the "one man, one vote" principle, this group is likely to assume control of the Republican party in the not too distant future.

Overall, given the trend of things, career-oriented individuals will increase and continue to dominate in the lawmaking body. This projection, it would seem, places new urgency on the obligation of students of politics to focus more clearly on the personal interests of formal decision-makers. While the literature of politics has stressed the special interests of groups, constituencies and parties, it has tended to ignore the fact that all these variables are linked through the office-holder as he pursues his own objectives. As such, this represents another important dimension to an understanding of the political process.

# Political Implications

In assessing a political system, various criteria are held up as guidelines. In American society, we use such standards as consent of the governed, government in the public interest, and a responsible two-party system. If these are the ideals, perhaps what is most needed at the present time is a critical examination of these terms to ascertain the extent to which they are in accord with the actual functioning of the polity.

# PROBLEM FOR DEMOCRACY: THE PUBLIC INTEREST AND THE PRIVATE INTEREST

In a democracy, it is generally accepted that the ultimate political authority is the people. Indeed, it is commonly taken for granted that the great virtue of a legislative institution is its representative quality which makes it more responsive to public needs than the other two branches of government.[4] Yet, if this concept is to possess meaning, it must be analyzed in operational terms. How effective are the means of control by which the people hold their representatives responsible for carrying out their will?

One of the important findings of this study is that primary and general elections have surprisingly little impact on the political careers of legislators. Even when defeated for re-election, which is infrequent, the incumbent is remarkably able to recoup his losses and resume his political pursuits. Of further significance is the fact that the ability of the lawmaker to survive and advance is very much dependent upon forces external to him, e.g., national election sweeps. On the rare occasion when he fails for re-election, it is usually because of nonpersonal factors, e.g., urban reform movements.

Under such conditions, the legislator has considerable leeway to pursue his particular objectives. Because accountability to the citizenry is tenuous, public interest considerations do not necessarily circumscribe him; particularly when they might be incompatible with his private interest. This was demonstrated by the surprisingly

---

4. For example: "Of all branches of government, the Legislature is closest to its constituency and is the largest group of representative officials directly responsible to the people. Its members are required to stand for election more often than any of the other coordinate branches." New York State Legislature, *Report of the Joint Legislative Committee on Practices and Procedures*, Leg. Doc. No. 21, Albany, 1959.

high percentage of legislators who were eventually caught compromising their honor.

Relevant to this, further, is the fact that legislators have been given the privilege of carrying on with their private business or profession while performing a public role; and, as was seen, they take full advantage of this. It seems, then, that there exists the kind of situation where the legislator might tend to confuse his public duties with his private responsibilities. To rectify this condition, legal and civic groups have urged that a new and stronger code of ethics be passed into law which would carefully regulate the affairs of these public servants. But the legislator-careerists have strongly resisted such proposals. To encourage and strengthen public control devices would be to jeopardize, as they see it, the very rationale of a political career: namely, the pursuit of the "prizes."

## THE FUNCTIONAL ROLE OF PARTY

In an article entitled "Toward Functionalism in Political Science," Theodore Lowi makes a plea for a functional approach to the study of political parties, i.e., "how parties are functionally related to the political system."[5] He contends that in analyzing the role of parties, mere inventories of their duties are not enough. To illustrate, most of us would agree that the task of selecting candidates and the running of election campaigns is one of the important responsibilities of party. But this alone tells us little about the possible consequences of this role upon the political system.[6] It is with this in mind that we have attempted to assess the two major parties as they operate in the New York State Legislature.

---

5. *The American Political Science Review* 57 (September, 1963): 570–83.

6. For a comprehensive explanation of this theoretical approach see Robert Merton, *Social Theory and Social Action* (Illinois: The Free Press of Glencoe, 1949), Chap. 1.

*The Democratic party*

An important role of party is to fulfill the special needs of certain groups in the population. Pertinent here is the kind of relationship that has developed between the "underdog" groups of the community and the Democratic party. For the Irish and other immigrant peoples who followed, the problem has been how to realize the proud boast of America that there is opportunity for all. Generally excluded from the conventional routes for advancement, the party provided them with alternative avenues of social mobility. With surprising regularity, it has led the newcomers to one of the most prestigeful positions available—the judgeship. In addition to providing this kind of special recognition, the party has also been the instrument through which the newer ethnic minorities have been introduced to positions of authority and a role in statewide policy-making. Not to be overlooked is that these gains have been lasting ones.

Significant, also, is the Democratic party's role in establishing a recruitment bridge between the legislature and the judicial branch. While it is the Democrats who have been most active in initiating and perpetuating this pattern, the Republicans have come to assume an active role here as well. Furthermore, the high regularity at which this recruitment practice occurs indicates that this too is now a standard feature of the political system.

If parties are functional to the political system, it is often the case that they prove to be dysfunctional as well; that is, they contribute to certain consequences, either intended or unintended, which have detrimental effects.[7] Party actions which might have been useful in the past may eventually reach the point of negative returns. While the Democratic organization has aided in the adjustment of lower status minority groups, it has come to impede

_____
7. *Ibid.,* pp. 153–155.

full adjustment by the almost total exclusion of Yankee stock from its ranks. Nor has it, as yet, given full recognition to the political aspirations of the newest minorities, e.g., the Negroes.

## The Republican party

By and large, the Republican organization has played a defensive role, one which is best calculated to preserve the interests of the established groups of society. Formerly a party which consisted almost entirely of white, Anglo-Saxon Protestants, it has since slowly opened its doors to those of other ethnic and religious groups. But this has come about only after the newcomers have themselves become established and manifested "respectability."

And while the Republican party has been home to those of Yankee background, as well as those who come closest to approximating it, the organization has at the same time provided succor to the moneyed and landed interests. Previously, it was the patrician-type executive and farmer who predominated. Since then, a greater number of the middle class and particularly lawyers have made entrance. But among all Republican groupings, there is evidence of continued extensive connections with banks, corporations, and property organizations, much more so than among the Democrats. In part, this helps explain why the Republican membership has not used the party for purposes of social and political mobility as exhaustively as the Democrats; the need is not as great.

Of course, it must not be forgotten that the party has led its members to places of authority within the legislature. Among the most important positions in the state are those of the Speaker of the Assembly, the Senate President Pro Tem and certain committee chairmanships. This helps to account for the party's strong fight to perpetuate legislative malapportionment. Up to the recent past, it was only through such manipulation that the upstate Republicans could hold on to power and distribute shares of it to deserving members. It was as much to the interest of this party to preserve malapportionment as it has been for the Democratic organization to deliver its members to extra-legislative seats of authority.

## PARTISAN WORLDS

Despite changes, wide divergencies still exist between the legislative members of both parties. Not only is there significant variation in the social backgrounds of the lawmakers, but, as we previously noted, there are important differences in their career perspectives as well. The Democrats look to the particular kinds of opportunities afforded by New York City and the Republicans depend upon the rest of the state. Rather than emphasizing elective competition, the concern has been: what is the most assured path to the rewards of political office? To quote from V. O. Key: ". . . the problem of American state politics is more one of keeping the politicians fighting among themselves than of avoiding damaging conflict."[8]

From out of this there arises the problem of the adequate provision of statewide leadership. There is evidence that despite the existence of a strong two-party system, the legislative parties are failing in this responsibility. They produce few personnel who exhibit the kind of experience and qualities that is attractive both to the voters of the metropolis and the upstate areas—over the past thirty-five years, no state legislator has been elected to such a leading statewide office as the governorship.

### Relations with the Governor

The partisan cleavage which exists in the legislature affects the political system in still other ways. In comparing the legislature with the executive branch, much has

8. V. O. Key, *American State Politics*, p. 274.

been made in the literature of politics about the relative shrinkage of legislative power. There are, of course, many reasons for this. Important is the fact that lawmakers possess neither the expertise nor the time to deal with the highly technical matters of the twentieth century; of necessity, such matters are delegated to administrators. But certainly just as significant is that it is the Governor who can pose as the great unifier; it is he who can claim to speak for the welfare of all the people of the state. Governors from Roosevelt to Rockefeller drew their strength largely from an ability to project such an image. The legislature on the other hand seems poorly equipped to provide consensus. No matter what the issue, the chances are that the same old tune will be played: New York City Democrats versus upstate Republicans.[9]

This is much the basis to the rivalry which exists between the executive and legislative branches of government. Legislative leaders often resist the Governor's stewardship, regardless of whether the Governor is of the same party or another. The very fact that he has superior public relations and can rally public opinion will cause resentment. As many see it, the desired goal is to establish more effective relationships between the Governor and the legislature;[10] and one useful technique with which the former can hope to accomplish this is through his control over patronage. By deciding who among the legislators is, or is not, to be appointed to an important position, the chief executive is able to consolidate his power.

Yet there is indication that Democratic Governors have been at a decided disadvantage in the use of this method. One prime reason is that malapportionment, during most of the years it was in effect, presented them with a Repub-

9. We can anticipate, however, that as suburban strength grows, there would develop some changes in the traditional alignments.

10. For example, the Committee on American Legislatures of the American Political Science Association in Belle Zeller, ed., *American State Legislatures* (New York: Thomas Y. Crowell Company, 1954), p. 167.

lican-controlled legislature which neither expected nor counted on appointments from Democrats. But we also see that Democratic executives can't even depend upon patronage as a means of influencing members of their own party. This is because many of the best positions sought by Democratic lawmakers are to be found in New York City; and they can be made available irrespective of the Governor's feelings. The chief executive must, therefore, nurture agreeable relations with the holders of power in New York City—in most instances the county leaders of the party—if he is to be effective as a policy-maker and leader. When Governor Harriman's alliance with Tammany leader De Sapio foundered, his leadership in the legislature and in the state began to disintegrate.[11]

Of further significance is the fact that the Republican Governors have also been limited in their use of patronage as it has reference to the lawmakers. As was noted, many of the most important and desirable political offices in the state can be found in the legislature. For the most part, it is the Republicans who have had access to these offices. To the extent that this party can no longer count on continued control of the legislature, which is quite likely because of reapportionment, the hand of any Republican Governor will probably be strengthened.

## LATENT ASPECTS OF LEGISLATIVE BEHAVIOR

Most people view the legislature as a forum where the lawmakers study, discuss, and formulate policy. In this context, it is the representative role which is usually emphasized. That is, the legislature is perceived as a body of elected delegates whose chief responsibility is to serve as spokesmen for their constituents. Yet there is little empirical evidence of the extent to which these delegates defer to their representative function.

---

11. Daniel P. Moynihan and James Q. Wilson analyze this further in their study "Patronage in New York State, 1955–59," pp. 286–301.

In his study of political representation, Alfred De Grazia discusses the matter:

> When an American thinks of representation, he generally thinks of his vote. It is his weapon and with it he can subdue any dragon that may emerge from the cave of political intrigue. From the vote he supposes, comes his government, and from the government, actions which generally purport to conform with his wishes. But if he ponders a little longer, he will remember feelings of frustration at certain acts of his representatives; he will recall the depths of his ignorance about the habits and characteristics of his representatives; and he will realize that his weapon, though a handy one, cannot assure his control of all the specialized operations required in government.[12]

What must be acknowledged is that a legislator is expected to perform many other roles in the political system which can and do conflict with his representative role. For example, we speak of the lawmaker as "broker," as "party member," or as "politician." These terms refer to the legislator's relations with his "clienteles," i.e., pressure groups, party organizations and officials in the administrative branch as well as constituents. "These clienteles maintain expectations concerning the legislator's behavior, expectations which he cannot escape without risk to the very position he occupies as a legislator."[13]

While the present study has attempted to treat these diverse roles, it is the legislator as a career politician which has been highlighted. Here, the lawmaker is perceived as one who has self-expectations from which he cannot escape; he is in politics not only to serve his constituents and diverse groups, but to help himself as well.

### The "careerist" role vis à vis other roles

To carry this one step further, it can generally be assumed that the legislator appraises his clienteles from a

---

12. *Public and Republic* (New York: Alfred A. Knopf, 1951), p. 1.
13. Wahlke, *et al., The Legislative System*, p. 243.

perspective of self-concern. In problems that come before him, the question likely to be asked is: "How does this affect my career?" A politician is likely to confer little or no importance to constituency or group expectations if such expectations will undermine or somehow limit his political career. This is to say, the "careerist" role will take precedence over other roles. This was observed among suburban personnel who, for many years, ignored underrepresentation of their home areas so as to avoid political competition and the anonymity which comes with additional lawmakers from the same county. This shows up again in the preoccupation of legislators with judicial rewards: because of this they have found it difficult to agree on how to expand and reorganize the state judiciary—a matter of some urgency in light of the growing legal needs of the public.

By the same token, the career perspective may accentuate other kinds of attachments. In a state where parties are reasonably strong, careers can be made or broken by the decisions of key party officials. This includes public officials who dispense patronage as well as county and district party leaders who ask for it. Thus, a major task for the legislator-careerist is to affiliate himself with that party grouping which would appear to do him the most good as a political professional. Once this affiliation is made, he must be prepared to adjust his ideas, opinions and even principles to the expectations of his fellow partisans. In New York, most lawmakers would sooner defer to party than to any other kind of affiliation.

## Manifest and latent consequences

It is with this in mind that we distinguish between "manifest" and "latent" consequences of behavior. The former has reference to those consequences which are intended and recognized; the latter pertains to that which is unintended and not recognized.[14] Both can either con-

14. This is developed by Robert K. Merton, pp. 19–84.

tribute to or detract from the working operations of an institution. By failing to discern the less obvious aspects of human affairs, however, we risk the kind of appraisal wherein unworkable remedies are proposed for important problems.

Actually, the notion of the legislature as a decisional system where constituency interests are weighed and policy alternatives carefully considered, can be misleading. A good deal of legislative behavior does not involve policy-making at all; and when a policy decision is finally made, it is not necessarily based on the merits of the issue as such. Indeed, the function that most of us take for granted, i.e., legislation, is largely incidental to the other activities of lawmakers. Certainly we cannot ignore their preoccupation with social and political mobility. Any suggestions which would change or "reform" the lawmaking institution must take this into account.

## RECOMMENDATIONS

We need our politicians and especially the careerists who accrue so much experience and dedicate so much of their life energies to public service. But we must also secure the conditions whereby public responsiveness and accountability can be assured. The key to this is to make the legislative process simpler and more visible. Our politicians must be seen and known, and wherever possible legislative practices must be so structured as to be understood by the many. Ultimately, and something which is more difficult to effect, the electorate must be prepared to act on what they see and hear. It is believed that the following recommendations go to the heart of the matter.

1. Now that the United States Supreme Court's "one-man, one vote" decision requires that Senate and Assembly shall be elected on the basis of population alone, a unicameral legislature should be adopted. It would thus be easier for the citizenry to focus responsibility, preclud-

ing a situation where one house "passes the buck" to the other. It would also be the means of reducing the number of lawmakers, giving each one greater prominence before the electorate.

2. New York is a large and highly diversified state that must face up to increasingly acute governmental problems. Urban redevelopment, highways, congested metropolitan areas, water and air pollution, school facilities, and public welfare are but some of the more important areas that must be treated by the lawmakers. No one man can absorb and understand all the complex issues by spending three or four months in the Capitol. Thus, the legislature should be a continuing body like the Congress and law-makers should be full-time employees as are public executives and judges. This arrangement, furthermore, would go a long way toward resolving some of the stickiest aspects of conflicts-of-interest.

3. A minimum of four-year terms should be instituted. As we have seen, frequent elections do not assure greater accountability. On the other hand, less frequent elections would help dissipate the redundancy of campaigns and thus encourage a more alert electorate. Furthermore, it would make for a continuously more experienced group of legislators relieved of the burden of running an expensive and time-consuming campaign every two years.

4. The persisting division of New York State into Republican upstate and Democratic New York City should be discouraged as it is not conducive to a competitive and responsible form of politics. It is recommended that proportional representation should be introduced as a method of electing legislators. Large districts, electing several members, could be set up on the basis of population and within each district the voter would indicate his order of choice. Thus each party would be assured of greater representation in all parts of the state.[15]

---

15. See Constitutional Revision Committee, *Citizens Union Position Paper No. 2* (Citizens Union of the City of New York, 1967).

As can be seen, there is no tinkering here with either non-partisan arrangements or with new and more restrictive forms of control. The proposals offered recognize that human nature changes slowly, at best, and the struggle for power cannot be contained. The idea, rather, is to direct political endeavor through such channels as are likely to lead toward more constructive public ends; or, as Madison explains in Federalist Paper Number 51, ". . . that the private interest of every individual may be a sentinel over the public rights." The ultimate goal is to make the legislature and the state more viable parts of the national system.

# BIBLIOGRAPHY

General References on Politics, Government,
History, and Sociology

*Books*

Adrian, Charles R. *Governing Urban America.* New
York: McGraw-Hill Book Company, 1961.
————. *State and Local Governments.* New York: Mc-
Graw-Hill Book Company, 1960.
Baker, Gordon E. *Rural Versus Urban Political Power.*
New York: Doubleday and Company, 1955.
Banfield, Edward C. (ed.). *Urban Government.* New
York: The Free Press of Glencoe, 1961.
Bell, Daniel. *The End of Ideology.* New York: Collier
Books, 1962.
Boskoff, Alvin. *The Sociology of Urban Regions.* New
York: Appleton-Century-Crofts, 1962.
Dahl, Robert. *Who Governs, Democracy and Power in an
American City.* New Haven, Conn. Yale University
Press, 1961.
Dewey, John. *The Public and Its Problems.* New York:
Henry Holt and Company, Inc., 1957.
Donovan, Robert J. *Eisenhower: The Inside Story.* New
York: Harper and Brothers, 1956.
Duncan, Otis D. and Albert J. Reiss, Jr. *Social Charac-
teristics of Urban and Rural Communities.* New
York: John Wiley and Sons.
Gerth, H. H. and C. Wright Mills (eds.). *From Max
Weber: Essays in Sociology.* New York: Oxford Uni-
versity Press, 1958.

197

Gross, Bertram M. *The Legislative Struggle: A Study in Social Combat.* New York: McGraw-Hill Book Company, 1953.

Handlin, Oscar. *The Newcomers.* Cambridge, Mass.: Harvard University Press, 1959.

Kaufman, Herbert. *Politics and Policies in State and Local Governments.* Englewood Cliffs, N.J.: Prentice-Hall, Inc., 1963.

Key, V. O. *American State Politics: An Introduction.* New York: Alfred A. Knopf, 1956.

———. *Politics, Parties and Pressure Groups.* New York: Thomas Y. Crowell, 1958.

———. *Public Opinion and American Democracy.* New York: Alfred A. Knopf, 1961.

Lasswell, Harold. *Politics: Who Gets What, When, How.* New York: McGraw-Hill Book Company, 1936.

Lasswell, Harold and Abraham Kaplan. *Power and Society, A Framework For Political Inquiry.* New Haven, Conn.: Yale University Press, 1925.

Lasswell, Harold, *et al. The Comparative Study of Elites.* Stanford, Calif.: Stanford University Press, 1952.

Lazarsfeld, Paul, *et al. The People's Choice.* New York: Columbia University Press, 1948.

Lipset, Seymour and Reinhard Bendix. *Social Mobility in Industrial Society.* Berkeley and Los Angeles: University of California Press, 1960.

Loomis, Charles P. and J. Allen Beegle. *Rural Social Systems.* Englewood Cliffs, N.J.: Prentice-Hall, 1950.

Lubell, Samuel. *The Future of American Politics.* New York: Doubleday and Company, 1956.

Marvick, Dwaine. *Political Decision-Makers.* New York: The Free Press of Glencoe, 1961.

Matthews, Donald R. *United States Senators and Their World.* Chapel Hill: University of North Carolina Press, 1960.

————. *The Social Background of Political Decision-Makers.* New York: Doubleday and Company, 1954.

Merton, Robert K. *Social Theory and Social Structure.* Illinois: The Free Press of Glencoe, 1949.

Ogburn, William F. *Social Characteristics of Cities.* Chicago: International City Manager's Association, 1955.

Pareto, V. I. *The Mind and Society.* Vol. 3. New York: Harcourt Brace and Company, 1935.

Pfiffner, John M. and Robert V. Presthus. *Public Administration.* New York: The Ronald Press, 1960.

Queen, Stuart A. and David B. Carpenter. *The American City.* New York: McGraw-Hill Book Company, 1953.

Reed, Alfred Z. *Training for the Public Profession of Law.* Bulletin #15. New York: Carnegie Foundation for the Advancement of Teaching, 1921.

————. *Present-Day Law Schools.* Bulletin #21. New York: Carnegie Foundation for the Advancement of Teaching, 1928.

Schattschneider, E. E. *The Semisovereign People, A Realist's View of Democracy in America.* New York: Holt, Rinehart and Winston, 1960.

Schlesinger, Arthur, Jr. *The Politics of Upheaval.* Boston: Houghton Mifflin and Company, 1960.

Schlesinger, Joseph. *How They Became Governor.* East Lansing, Mich.: Michigan State University, 1957.

————. *Ambition and Politics: Political Careers in the United States.* Chicago: Rand McNally and Company, 1966.

Schubert, Glendon. *The Public Interest.* New York: The Free Press of Glencoe, 1960.

Shubik, Martin. *Readings in Game Theory and Political Behavior.* New York: Doubleday and Company, Inc., 1954.

Truman, David B. *The Governmental Process.* New York: Alfred A. Knopf, 1957.

Wahlke, John C., *et al. The Legislative System.* New York: John Wiley and Sons, 1962.

Warner, W. Lloyd, *et al. Democracy in Jonesville.* New York: Harper and Brothers, 1949.

Warner, W. Lloyd and Paul S. Lunt. *The Social Life of a Modern Community.* New Haven, Conn.: Yale University Press, 1941.

Williams, Oliver P. and Charles Press. *Democracy in Urban America.* Chicago: Rand McNally and Company, 1961.

Wood, Robert C. *Suburbia, Its People and Their Politics.* Boston: Houghton Mifflin Company, 1959.

Zeller, Belle. *American State Legislatures.* New York: Thomas Y. Crowell Company, 1954.

*Articles*

Bell, Wendell. "Social Structure and Participation in Different Types of Formal Associations," *Social Forces* 34 (May, 1956) : 345–50.

Brown, John Mason. "The State Legislature as Training for Further Public Service," *Annals of the American Academy of Political and Social Sciences* 195 (January, 1938) : 176–82.

Duncan, Otis D., "The Optimum Size of Cities," *Cities and Society,* Paul K. Hatt and Albert J. Reiss, eds. Glencoe, Ill.: The Free Press of Glencoe, 1957. Pp. 759–72.

Edwards, Alba E. "A Socio-Economic Grouping of the Gainful Workers in the United States," *Journal of the American Statistical Association* 28 (December, 1933) : 377–87.

Eulau, Heinz and David Koff. "Occupational Mobility and Political Career," *The Western Political Quarterly* 15 (September, 1962) , 507–21.

Eulau, Heinz, *et al.* "Career Perspectives of American State Legislators," in *Political Decision Makers,*

Dwaine Marvick, ed. New York: The Free Press of Glencoe, 1961. Pp. 218–63.

Fiellin, Alan. "Recruitment and Legislative Role Conceptions: A Conceptual Scheme and a Case Study," *The Western Political Quarterly* 20 (June, 1967), 271–87.

Hyneman, Charles S. "Tenure and Turnover of Legislative Personnel," *Annals of the American Academy of Political and Social Science* 195 (January, 1938): 21–31.

————. "Who Makes Our Laws?" *Political Science Quarterly* 55 (December, 1940): 556–81.

Jewell, Malcolm E. "Party Voting in American State Legislatures," *The American Political Science Review* 49 (September, 1955): 773–91.

Jonassen, Christen T. "Community Typology," in *Community Structure Analysis,* Marvin B. Sussman, ed. New York: Thomas Y. Crowell, 1959. Pp. 15–36.

Kahl, Joseph A. and James A. Davis. "A Comparison of Indexes of Socio-Economic Status," *The American Sociological Review* 20 (June, 1955): 317–25.

Komarovsky, Mirra. "The Voluntary Association of Urban Dwellers," *The American Sociological Review* 11 (December, 1946): 686–98.

Latham, Earl. "The Group Basis of Politics: Notes for a Theory," *The American Political Science Review* 46 (June, 1952).

Lowi, Theodore. "Toward Functionalism in Political Science: The Case of Innovation in Party Systems," *The American Political Science Review* 57 (September, 1963): 570–83.

Reiss, Albert J., Jr. "The Sociological Study of Communities," *Rural Sociology* 24 (June, 1959): 118–30.

Rosenzweig, Robert M. "The Politician and the Career in Politics," *Midwest Journal of Political Science* 1 (August, 1957): 163–72.

Schlesinger, Joseph A. "Lawyers and American Politics:

A Clarified View," *Midwest Journal of Political Science* 1 (May, 1957): 26–39.

Schnore, Leo F. and David Varley. "Some Concomitants of Metropolitan Size," *The American Sociological Review* 20 (August, 1955): 408–19.

Seligman, Lester G. "The Study of Political Leadership," *The American Political Science Review* 15 (December, 1950): 904–15.

———. "A Prefatory Study of Leadership Selection in Oregon," *Western Political Quarterly* 12 (March, 1959): 153–67.

Shils, Edward A. "The Legislator and His Environment," *University of Chicago Law Review* 18 (Spring, 1951).

Whyte, William F. "Social Organization in the Slums," *The American Sociological Review* 8 (February, 1943): 34–39.

Woodward, J. L. and E. Roper. "Political Activity of American Citizens," *The American Political Science Review* 44 (December, 1950): 872–85.

Wright, Charles R. and Herbert H. Hyman: "Voluntary Association Memberships of American Adults: Evidence From National Sample Surveys," *American Sociological Review* 23 (June, 1958): 284–94.

*Documents*

United States Bureau of the Census. *Census of Population: 1950. Number of Inhabitants.* Vol. I. Washington: Government Printing Office, 1952.

———. *Fifteenth Census of the United States: 1930. Population,* Vol. III. Washington: Government Printing Office, 1932.

———. *Nativity and Parentage, United States Census of Population: 1950.* Washington: Government Printing Office, 1952.

———. *Religious Bodies: 1936.* Vol. I. Washington: Government Printing Office, 1941.

———. *Seventeenth Census of the United States: 1950.*

*Population.* Vol. II, Part 32. Washington: Government Printing Office, 1952.

————. *U. S. Census of Governments: 1957. Government in New York.* Vol. VI, No. 30. Washington: Government Printing Office, 1959.

United States Census Office. *Tenth Census: 1880.* Population Schedules. Washington: National Archives Microfilm Publications.

United States Commission on Intergovernmental Relations. *A Report to the President for Transmittal to the Congress.* Washington: Government Printing Office, 1955.

### Unpublished Materials

Keys, Fenton. "The Correlation of Social Phenomena with Community Size." Unpublished Ph.D. Dissertation, Yale University, New Haven, 1942.

Paster, Howard G. "Ethics in Albany." Unpublished Master's Thesis, Columbia University, New York, 1967.

### Special References on New York City and New York State

### Books

Adams, Thomas. *The Building of the City.* Vol. 1. New York: Regional Plan of New York and Its Environs, 1929.

Adams, Thomas, *et al. Population, Land Values and Government.* New York: Regional Plan of New York and Its Environs, 1929.

Berelson, Bernard *et al. Voting: A Study of Opinion Formation in a Presidential Campaign.* Chicago: The University of Chicago Press, 1954.

Caldwell, Lynton K. *The Government and Administration of New York.* New York: Thomas Y. Crowell Company, 1954.

Costikyan, Edward N. *Behind Closed Doors*. New York: Harcourt, Brace and World, 1966.

Ellis, David M., *et al. A Short History of New York State*. Ithaca, N.Y.: Cornell University Press, 1957.

Flynn, Edward J. *You're the Boss: The Practice of American Politics*. New York: The Viking Press, 1947.

Gartrell, Leland. *Religious Affiliation—New York City and Metropolitan Region*. New York: Protestant Council of the City of New York, 1958 (mimeographed).

Glazer, Nathan and Daniel Patrick Moynihan. *Beyond the Melting Pot: The Negroes, Puerto Ricans, Jews, Italians, and Irish of New York City*. Cambridge, Mass.: The M.I.T. press and Harvard University Press, 1963.

Hoover, Edgar M. and Raymond Vernon. *Anatomy of a Metropolis*. Cambridge, Mass.: Harvard University Press, 1959.

Lowi, Theodore J. *At The Pleasure of the Mayor*. New York: The Free Press of Glencoe, 1964.

Moscow, Warren. *Politics in the Empire State*. New York: Alfred A. Knopf, 1948.

Peel, Roy V. *The Political Clubs of New York City*. New York: G. P. Putnam's Sons, 1935.

Riordan, William L. *Plunkitt of Tammany Hall*. New York: Alfred A. Knopf, 1948.

Sayre, Wallace S. and Herbert Kaufman. *Governing New York City*. New York: Russell Sage Foundation, 1960.

Straetz, Ralph A. and Frank K. Munger. *New York Politics*. New York: New York University Press, 1960.

Vidich, Arthur J. and Joseph Bensman. *Small Town in Mass Society*. Princeton, N.J.: Princeton University Press, 1958.

Zeller, Belle. *Pressure Politics in New York*. New York: Prentice-Hall, Inc., 1937.

*Articles*

Bone, Hugh A. "Political Parties in New York City," *American Political Science Review* 40 (April, 1946) : 272–82.

Lederle, John W. "New York's Legislature Under the Microscope." *American Political Science Review,* 40 (June, 1946) : 521–27.

Moynihan, Daniel P. and James Q. Wilson. "Patronage in New York State, 1955–59," *American Political Science Review* 58 (June, 1964) : 286–301.

Silva, Ruth C. "Apportionment of the New York State Legislature," *American Political Science Review* 55 (December, 1961) : 870–81.

Spivack, Robert G. "New York Backslides," in *Our Sovereign State,* Robert S. Allen, ed. New York: The Vanguard Press, 1949. Pp. 69–95.

Tyler, Gus and David I. Wells. "New York Constitutionally Republican," in *The Politics of Reapportionment.* Malcolm E. Jewell, ed. New York: Atherton Press, 1962. Pp. 221–48.

*Documents and Guides*

Institute of Judicial Administration. *A Guide to Court Systems.* The Institute, New York, 1960.

*McKinney's Consolidated Laws of New York.* Brooklyn, New York: Edward Thompson Company, 1944. Annual Supplements.

New York Assembly. *The Assembly: Genesis, Evolution and History.* Albany, 1960.

New York City. *The City of New York Official Directory* ("Green Book"). New York: The City Record. Published annually.

New York City. Health Department. Deaths Plus Still-Births Reported, 1888–1956.

*New York Red Book.* Albany. Published Annually.

New York State, Joint Legislative Committee on Legislative Methods, Procedures and Expenditures. *Final Report*. Albany: Williams Press, 1946.

————, Joint Legislative Committee to Investigate the Affairs of the City of New York. *Report to the Legislature*. December 28, 1932.

————, Secretary of State. *Manual for the Use of the Legislature of the State of New York*. Albany: Williams Press, 1843–. Published annually.

New York State Legislature. *Report of the Joint Legislative Practices and Procedures*. Leg. Doc. No. 21. Albany, 1959.

Rankin, Rebecca B. *Guide to the Municipal Government of the City of New York*. New York: Record Press, 1952.

State of New York. *Report of the Assembly Committee on Ethics and Guidance*. Leg. Doc. No. 12. Albany, 1962.

## Biographical Sources

*Directories*

*The American Catholic Who's Who*. Grosse Point, Michigan: Walter Romig-Publisher, issued biennially, 1934–1960.

*The American Catholic Who's Who, 1911*. St. Louis, Mo.: B. Herder, 1911.

*American Woman; the Official Who's Who Among the Women of the Nation*. Los Angeles: American Publications, Inc., 1935–36.

*America's Young Men; the Official Who's Who Among the Young Men of the Nation*. Los Angeles: American Publications, Inc., 1934, 1936–37, 1938–39.

*Biographical Directory of the State of New York*. New York, 1900.

*The Brown Book: A Biographical Record of Public Officials of the City of New York for 1898–99.* New York: M. B. Brown and Company, 1899.

*Italian American Who's Who.* New York: The Vigo Press, issued annually, 1920–1963.

New York State. *The New York Red Book.* Albany, N.Y.: Published annually from 1892.

Nowinson, Richard, ed., *Who's Who in United States Politics and American Political Almanac.* Chicago: Capital House, 1950.

Queens County, New York. *Portrait and Biographical Record of Queens County.* New York and Chicago: Chapman Publishing Company, 1950.

*Who's Who in American Jewry.* New York: National News Association, 1926, 1927 and 1938.

*Who's Who in Colored America.* New York: Who's Who in Colored America, 2 vols., 1927 and 1938–40.

*Who's Who in Commerce and Industry.* New York: A. N. Marquis, issued serially, 1936–.

*Who's Who in Engineering.* Lewis Historical Publishing Company, Inc. Issued serially from 1922.

*Who's Who in Government.* New York: The Biographical Research Bureau, Inc., 1930, 1932.

*Who's Who in Labor.* New York: The Dryden Press, 1946.

*Who's Who in New York* (city and state). Who's Who Publications, Inc. Issued biennially, 1904–14; periodically 1918–60.

*Who's Who in Queens.* Jamaica, New York, 1936.

*Who's Who in the East.* Boston: Larkin, Roosevelt & Larkin, 1942–43; Chicago: Marquis, 1955.

*Who's Who in World Jewry; a Biographical Directory of Outstanding Jews.* Who's Who in Jewry, Inc., 1955.

*Who's Who in Westchester County.* Hastings-on-Hudson, New York; Hastings News, 1931.

*Histories and Genealogies*

*Biographical History of Westchester County, New York.* Chicago: Lewis Historical Publishing Company, 1899.

Chase, Franklin Henry. *Syracuse and Its Environs.* vols. 2, 3. New York and Chicago: Lewis Historical Publishing Company, Inc., 1924.

Cutter, William R., ed. *Genealogical and Family History of Western New York.* 3 vols. New York: Lewis Historical Publishing Company, 1912.

Doty, Lockwood R., ed. *History of the Genesee Country.* Chicago: S. J. Clarke Publishing Company, 1925.

Doty, William I., ed. *The Historic Annals of Southwestern New York.* vol. 3. New York: Lewis Historical Publishing Company, Inc., 1940.

Downs, John P., ed. *History of Chautauqua County and Its People.* vol. 3. New York: American Historical Society, Inc., 1921.

Fitch, Charles E. *Encyclopedia of Biography of New York.* 8 vols. New York: American Historical Society, 1916–1925.

Fort Orange Recording Bureau. *Prominent People of the Capital District.* Albany, 1923.

French, Alvin P., ed. *History of Westchester County.* vols. 3, 4, 5. New York and Chicago: Lewis Historical Publishing Company, Inc., 1925.

Galpin, William F. *Central New York: An Island Empire.* New York: Lewis Historical Publishing Company, Inc., 1941.

Greene, Nelson, ed. *History of the Mohawk Valley, Gateway to the West, 1914–1925.* vols. 3, 4. Chicago: S. J. Clarke Publishing Company, 1925.

Greene, Nelson, ed. *History of the Valley of the Hudson.* vols. 3, 4. Chicago: The S. J. Clarke Publishing Company, 1931.

Griffin, Ernest Freeland. *Westchester County and Its Peo-*

*ple, A Record.* vol. 3. New York: Lewis Historical Publishing Company, Inc., 1946.

Hayner, Rutherford. *Troy & Rensselaer County New York, A History.* vol. III. New York and Chicago: Lewis Historical Publishing Company, 1925.

Hazelton, Henry I. *The Boroughs of Brooklyn and Queens, Counties of Nassau and Suffolk, Long Island, New York, 1609–1924.* 3 vols. New York: Lewis Historical Publishing Company, Inc., 1925.

Hill, Henry Wayland. *Municipality of Buffalo, New York, A History.* vols. 3, 4. New York and Chicago: Lewis Historical Publishing Company, Inc., 1923.

Horton, John T. and Edward T. Williams. *History of North Western New York.* vol. 3. New York: Lewis Historical Publishing Company, Inc., 1947.

Kimball, Francis P. *The Capital Region of New York State.* New York: Lewis Historical Publishing Company, Inc., 1942.

Lamb, Wallace E. *The Lake Champlain and Lake George Valleys.* New York: The American Historical Company, 1940.

Landon, Harry Fay. *The North Country.* vols. 2, 3. Indianapolis, Indiana: Historical Publishing Company, 1932.

Leng, Charles William and William T. Davis. *Staten Island and Its People, 1609–1929.* vols. 3, 4. New York: Lewis Historical Publishing Company, 1933.

McGuire, James K., ed. *The Democratic Party of the State of New York.* vol. 3. New York: United States History Company, 1905.

*Men of Affairs in New York: An Historical Work.* New York: L. R. Hamersley and Company, 1906.

Morris, Charles. *Men of Affairs in New York: An Historical Work.* New York: L. R. Hamersley and Company, 1906.

Seward, William Foote. *Binghamton and Broome County*

*New York, A History.* vol. 3. New York and Chicago: Lewis Historical Publishing Company, 1924.

Sullivan, James, ed. *History of New York State.* vol. 6. New York and Chicago: Lewis Historical Publishing Company, 1927.

Wells, James L., Louis F. Haffen, and Josia A. Briggs, eds. *The Bronx and Its People, A History, 1609–1927.* vols. 3, 4. New York: The Lewis Historical Publishing Company, 1927.

Wilner, Merton M. *Niagara Frontier.* vols. 3, 4. Chicago: The S. J. Clarke Publishing Company, 1931.

Zinn, Louise H., *et al., Southeastern New York.* vol. 3. New York: Lewis Historical Publishing Company, Inc., 1946.

## *Unpublished Materials*

Davenport, Frederick M. "Reminiscences." Columbia University Oral History Collection, Special Collections, Butler Library.

Teller Ludwig. "Reminiscences." Columbia University Oral History Collection, Special Collections, Butler Library.

The Bert Lord Papers. Collection of Regional History and University Archives, Cornell University.

## *New York State Newspapers*

*Advertiser* (Elmira). Published since 1853.

*Argus* (Mt. Vernon). Published since 1892.

*Brooklyn Eagle* (Brooklyn). Published 1841 to 1955.

*Citizen-Register* (Ossining). Published since 1840.

*Citizen-Advertiser* (Auburn). Published since 1870.

*Courier-Express* (Buffalo). Published since 1834.

*Democrat and Chronicle* (Rochester). Published since 1833.

*Freeman* (Kingston). Published since 1871.

*Gazette* (Niagara Falls). Published since 1854.

*Gazette* (Schenectady). Published since 1894.

*Herald-Journal* (Syracuse). Published since 1829.

*Herald-Tribune* (New York). Published 1841 to 1966.

*Journal* (Ithaca). Published since 1815.

*Journal* (Poughkeepsie). Published since 1882.

*Knickerbocker News* (Albany). Published since 1842.

*Leader* (Corning). Published since 1847.

*Leader-Herald* (Gloversville). Published since 1887.

*Long Island Press* (Jamaica). Published since 1889.

*New York Times.* Published since 1851.

*News* (Batavia). Published since 1878.

*News* (Buffalo). Published since 1834.

*News* (Newburgh). Published since 1885.

*Observer-Dispatch* (Utica). Published since 1922.

*Palladium Times* (Oswego). Published since 1819.

*Perry Herald* (Perry). Published since 1877.

*Post* (New York). Published since 1801.

*Post-Journal* (Jamestown). Published since 1826.

*Post-Standard* (Syracuse). Published since 1829.

*Post-Star* (Glen Falls). Published since 1904.

*Press* (Binghamton). Published since 1904.

*Press-Republican* (Plattsburgh). Published since 1895.

*Queens Evening News* (Long Island City). Published since 1915.

*Record* (Troy). Published since 1896.

*Recorder* (Amsterdam). Published since 1879.

*Saratogian* (Saratoga Springs). Published since 1854.

*Sentinel* (Rome). Published since 1821.

*Standard* (Cortland). Published since 1867.

*Star* (Peekskill). Published since 1922.

*Star-Gazette* (Elmira). Published since 1828.

*Star-Journal* (Long Island City). Published since 1841.

*Telegram* (Elmira). Published since 1879.

*Times* (Geneva). Published since 1895.

*Times* (Glen Falls). Published since 1879.

*Times* (Watertown). Published since 1861.

*Times Herald* (Olean). Published since 1860.

*Times Herald-Record* (Middletown). Published since 1851.

*Times-Record* (Troy). Published since 1899.

*Times-Union* (Albany). Published since 1856.

*Times-Union* (Rochester). Published since 1826.

*Union-Star* (Schenectady). Published since 1855.

*Union-Sun & Journal* (Lockport). Published since 1821.

*World Telegram and Sun* (New York). Published since 1867.

# INDEX

Appointments, 106, 107, 112, 113, 116, 117, 119, 123, 125, 126, 190
Aristotle: on rulers, 22

Bell, Daniel, 65, 66
Board of Social Welfare, 123
Brydges, Earl W., 155

Carlino, Joseph, 95, 96n, 155
Class status: legislators compared to fathers, 59–62; legislators compared to New York population, 66–68
Code of Ethics, 88, 94–96; 186. *See also* Lockwood Committee, and Laporte, Cloyd
Commission on Inter-Governmental Relations, 41
Committees, 153, 160–63. *See also* Rules Committee
Conflicts of interest: defined, 75. *See also* Code of Ethics
Corruption, 88–92. *See also* "Honest graft" and Code of Ethics
Costikyan, Edward, 104, 105
Court of Claims, 95
Croker, Richard, 134

Davis, Kingsley: on city life and social mobility, 34
Declaration of Independence, 107
De Grazia, Alfred, 192

Democratic party: constituency base of, 50; legislator characteristics of, 50, 51; ethnic recruitment in, 63–66; class, 69–72; political ethic of, 73; officers among legislators, 82; corruption in, 90, 91; *vs.* La Guardia, 120; and Tammany Hall, 121; impact of Irish, 135; career politicians in, 135, 136; functional role of, 187, 188; *See also* Seabury investigations
Democratic Theory, 1, 107; and representative government, 109–11; of Patrons, 130, 131, 185
De Sapio, Carmine, 191
Dewey, Thomas E., 93, 95, 119, 167–71, 177
Donovan, Robert, 118
Duryea, Perry B., 155

Eisenhower, Dwight D., 103, 116–18
Election defeats, 98, 99, 103–7
Eulau, Heinz, 139, 179

Farley, James A., 116, 117, 135
Farmers in the legislature, 68, 87
Federalist Paper Number 51, 196
Fiellin, Alan, 179
Flynn, Ed, 65, 116, 117
Fox, Dixon Ryan, 63

Fusion party, 106, 120

"Gain" politicians, 91
"Game" politicians, 91
Gannett, Frank E., 170
Glazer, Nathan, 135
Goldwater, Barry, 103
Governor of New York, 123, 125, 126, 128, 189–91. *See also* Harriman, Averell; Lehman, Herbert; Rockefeller, Nelson; Roosevelt, Franklin D.; Smith, Al

Handlin, Oscar, 58
Hanley, Joe R., 165–71, 176–78
Harriman, Averell, 119, 123, 133, 191
Hatch Act, 89, 89n
Heck, Oswald, 155
Hofstadter, Richard, 72, 73
"Honest graft," 92, 92n

Immigration history, 57–59, 65
Interest groups, 78–81; business and banking, 83–86
Ives, Irving M., 129, 152

Jacksonian democracy, 108
Johnson, Lyndon B., 175
Judiciary, 122, 126, 127, 144, 145, 149

Kaufman, Herbert, 142, 143, 145
Kennedy, Robert F., 173, 177
Key, V. O., 71, 72, 81, 103, 129, 189

Labor organizations, 80, 135, 172
La Guardia, Fiorello H., 106, 120
Laporte, Cloyd, 95
Lasswell, Harold: theory of political elites, 25, 26; on corruption, 91
Lawyers: predominance of, 68, 69, 87; law schools attended, 70–72; disbarment of, 88; careers of, 139–51
Legislative apportionment: in New York State, 35–38; effects on tenure, 45, 46; effects on party, 50; and single district system, 109, 120n; effects on counties, 121; effects on Patrons, 134; effects on career politicians, 137; effects on leadership, 163; effects on Governor, 190, 191
Legislative deadlock: 1965, 173
Legislative districts: different types, 34, 35; and representation, 38; and lawyer distribution, 146. *See also* Legislative apportionment
Legislative leaders, 153–60. *See also* Speaker, Majority Leader, and President Pro Tem
Legislative roles, 21, 192, 193
Lehman, Herbert H., 118
Liberal party, 172
Lindsay, John V., 173
Lobbying, 83, 84, 86
Lockwood Committee, 94
Lowi, Theodore, 43, 186
Lubell, Samuel, 57, 72

Machold, H. Edmund, 154
Macy, W. Kingsland, 169, 177
Mahoney, Walter, 155
Majority Leader, 153–55, 173
Malapportionment: *See* Legislative apportionment
Mayor of New York City, 113, 120, 126. *See also* La Guardia, Fiorello H., and Lindsay, John V.
McGinnies, Joseph A., 154
Metcalf, George, 97
Mosca, Gaetano: theory of the ruling class, 22–25
Moscow, Warren, 81, 82, 154

Moynihan, Daniel P., 119, 135

"New breed" politicians, 136, 137
New Deal, 67, 118, 135, 167
New York City: apportionment of legislators, 35–38; party clubs in, 42, 43; Democratic representation from, 48–50; legislator affiliations in, 80, 81; voters, 110; ethnic discrimination, 114; career opportunities, 119, 120; county government, 121; Board of Estimate, 121; administrative positions in, 126; importance of judiciary, 127; career politicians from, 134–36; Corporation Counsel's office in, 142, 143; distribution of lawyers from, 146–51; careerists from, 182–83; and the Governor, 191; and the Democratic party, 195. *See also* Seabury investigations
New York State Assembly: apportionment of, 36; as originally instituted, 108; terms of office, 109
New York State Constitutional Convention: of 1894, 36; of 1821, 108; of 1846, 108; of 1967, 174
New York State Senate: apportionment of, 36; as originally instituted, 108

O'Connell organization, 121
Organizational leadership, 80, 81

Pareto, Vilfredo: theory of ruling elites, 24–26
Party clubs, 42, 43, 114, 143, 144
Party leadership, 81–83
Personality system, 91
Plato: on rulers, 22
Platt, Thomas C., 85
Plunkitt, George Washington, 134

President Pro Tem, 153–55, 167, 188
Primary elections, 99
Property qualifications, 108
Proportional representation, 195

Reed, Alfred Z., 70, 71
Religious affiliation, 58, 64
Reform, 105, 106, 136
Representative role, 191, 192
Republican party: constituency base, 50, 51; legislator characteristics of, 50, 51; the Yankee hegemony, 63; class, 69–72; political ethic, 73; officers among legislators, 82; business connections of, 85, 86; corruption in, 91, 92; Patrons in, 131–34; careerists in, 136, 137; functional role of, 188, 189
Resignations, 99–102
Rockefeller, Nelson, 125, 126, 174, 190
Rogow, Arnold, 91
Roosevelt, Franklin D., 115–18, 128, 133, 135, 152, 190
Roosevelt, Theodore, 152
Roper and Associates survey, 110
Rules Committee, Assembly, 153

Salaries of legislators, 46–48, 83
Savings Bank Association of New York State, 86
Sayre, Wallace S., 142, 143, 145
Schlesinger, Joseph, 111, 142, 175, 176
Seabury investigations, 90, 105–106
Seligman, Lester: on careers of state legislators, 29
Shils, Edward A., 60, 61
Smith, Al, 105, 152
Speaker, 153–55, 161, 173, 175, 178, 188

Sprague, John D., 139
Suburbs: development in New York State, 52; legislator characteristics in, 53–55; career-politicians from, 137, 183–84

Ten Year Club, 45
Terms of office, 108, 109, 195
Thayer, Warren T., 84
Travia, Anthony J., 171–78

Upstate: rural apportionment in, 35–38; Republican representation in, 48–50; legislator affiliations in, 80, 81; voters in, 110; the Old Guard in, 154; Patrons from, 180–82; Republican party in, 195. *See also* Republican party
Voting studies, 112. *See also* Roper and Associates survey

Wadswoth, James W., Jr., 152
Wagner, Robert F., Sr., 152
Weber, Max, 68, 69, 129, 134
Whyte, William F., 90
Wilson, James Q., 119, 136, 138
Wilson, Woodrow, 19, 20, 103
*WMCA, Inc. v. Lomenzo, Secretary of State of New York,* 37, 163. *See also* Legislative apportionment

Zaretski, Joseph, 173
Zeller, Belle, 83, 84